My First Protest / Walkout

"When I was in fourth grade, we had what was called a 'sharing day.' The other kids all brought in their favorite toy or flowers from their garden, or they talked about what they did in the summertime, or they read a poem. . . . When I got up to the front of the room to share, this is what I shared: 'You guys are stupid, and this school is stupid, and I'm going home.' And I walked home, in the middle of the school day.

"When my grandmother asked me why I was home so early, I told her—and she fell on her ass, laughing. When my mom heard about it, she fell on her ass, too.

"My family rewarded that kind of independent behavior; they loved an individualist. Boy, if they only knew what was ahead of them."

—Cher in *THE FIRST TIME*

The First Time

CHER

AS TOLD TO
JEFF COPLON

POCKET BOOKS

New York London Toronto Sydney Tokyo Singapore

POCKET BOOKS, a division of Simon & Schuster Inc.
1230 Avenue of the Americas, New York, NY 10020

Copyright © 1998 by Isis Productions, Inc.

Originally published in hardcover in 1998 by Simon & Schuster Inc.

ISBN: 0-671-03488-X

First Pocket Books trade paperback printing August 1999

10 9 8 7 6 5 4 3

POCKET and colophon are registered trademarks of Simon & Schuster Inc.

Cover design by Jackie Seow
Cover photo by Michael Lavine/Edge; hand-lettering by Bernard Maisner

Printed in the U.S.A.

Page 272 constitutes an extension of the copyright page.

I want to thank
Michael Korda, my editor,
for having the most patience
of any man in this century.

For Son ⌐

The First Time

*Here my mom had to hold me up
so I could hit my high notes!*

My First Memory

I was four years old and living in Laurel Canyon.
I was a shy and introverted little girl, but sometimes I could be adventurous. My favorite game was hide-and-seek with Maria, the young Mexican girl who took care of me. We played in a little wooded area near my house.

One day while I was hiding—I was a very good hider!—I suddenly realized that I was lost. No sign of Maria anywhere. It was late in the afternoon, and already starting to get dark and shadowy, especially for someone who's only knee-high. My little patch of trees looked to me like the forest in *The Wizard of Oz,* where Dorothy gets freaked out by the lions and tigers and bears (oh my!), and the trees had those huge, long, bony, fingery branches.

I started calling, "Maria! Maria!" I wasn't crying yet, though, I was being brave, but I was really scared out of my little size-4 cotton underpants. It seemed like I was lost for days but it was probably more like half an hour—you can see that I was already becoming a little Drama Queen.

That this is my first memory is pretty scary in itself. But there you go! ⌒୦

My First Fear

—or—

Sigmund, Have I Got a (Four-Year-Old) Girl for You

I hated to be left with a baby-sitter. One night my mother and stepfather were going out to a party (and what babes they were!). Out of nowhere, I threw this enormous tantrum. But when I think about it, it wasn't really a tantrum. I was genuinely heartbroken and terrified. I thought that if they went out that door, they would never come back, and I would be alone in this gray nothingness void for eternity. (You know . . . something like Congress.)

My poor parents—what a way to start a romantic evening. I cried and cried until I fell into a very small heap on the floor. Even while I was screaming, I thought to myself, *What's the matter with you? Why are you going through all of this? This is silly.*

But I couldn't stop. You don't have to be a rocket scientist to realize that at the tender age of four I'd already lost a couple of cards out of my original pack of fifty-two! —◯

My First Movie
—or—
I'm Ready for My Close-up, "Pluto"!

When I turned four, my parents took me to see <u>Dumbo,</u> and I was never quite the same. We went into a huge palace called Grauman's Chinese Theatre, where there were young people dressed in Chinese costumes, waiting at the doors to take our tiny bits of paper and tear them in half. As we walked through the doors, I saw a sight that can only be described as nirvana: a colossal mountain of candy! But what was even more astounding was that the Chinese teenagers were just giving the candy away to anyone who walked up to them. *My God, this movie thing is heaven!*

Then one of the boys, who was carrying a flashlight, asked to look at our little piece of paper. He shined his flashlight at it and said, "Come this way." We went with him into the biggest room I'd ever seen. Up in the front, there was a stage so big that Godzilla could have tap-danced on it, with beautiful golden curtains.

We sat in the dark. The huge golden curtains magically rose and the movie started! It was in color; I'd never seen color! It was huge, and there were all these characters scampering around. I was mesmerized. When the circus animals started singing and dancing, that was it for me. I was a goner. I didn't know it wasn't real. I was in the movie, right along with those elephants and crows. *I want to do that,* I thought. That was my first career ambition: to be a star in animated films.

We were well into the movie when I realized I needed to go to the bathroom. At first I thought I could just hold it. Then I knew I couldn't, but I wasn't about to get up and go to the bathroom, because

I didn't want to miss a second of *Dumbo*. I made a conscious decision: I just wasn't going to get up from my seat.

So I peed in my pants. I gave up everything for my art! (Something I would come to regret in later years.)

My First Friends
—or—
Cher, Why Do Your Little Playmates Have Stubble?

I was a strange little girl. I was either really smiling or really morose. Sometimes I'd go off by myself just to sit in my room, and be private and quiet (of course I was only three and a half at the time).

During the day, when I stayed at Mamaw's (one of my grandmothers) with no one to play with, I often lived in my head. I would sit under her lemon tree with my two invisible friends, Sam and Pete. They were both truck drivers, although Pete looked more like a lumberjack to me, with his black-and-red-checked shirt and hat with flappy things over the ears.

We would pick the delicious cherry tomatoes growing on vines along a wall of Mamaw's house, and Sam and Pete and I would have tomato parties. And tea parties, too, with three cups and a real teapot, except my tea was lemonade. My friends and I would have long conversations about everything—what I liked, what I didn't like. I have to tell you that Sam and Pete were as *real* to me as Jimmy Stewart's Harvey was to him.

Well, needless to say, my mother was bereft. Entirely freaked out. Here she had this beatnik toddler who talked to imaginary friends who were grown men with stubble. Though she didn't tell me then, she wanted to take me to see a psychiatrist. But Mamaw said, "Don't be ridiculous." My grandmother understood me: I was just terribly lonely. ∽◯

The First Time My Mom Kicked Ass for Me

I remember it like it happened last week. It was a Saturday and I was sitting with my shaggy mutt, named Blackie, watching my mom get ready to go to work. She was playing Queen Anne of Austria in the play *The Three Musketeers*. She was getting ready to do a matinee. I remember how long it took her to pile her waist-length hair up in these elaborate curls, like Marie Antoinette. After she finished getting dressed, my mom let Blackie out to pee before putting him back inside for the afternoon.

Living next door to us was a Swedish masseuse who was also the neighborhood busybody. She was an uglier meaner-looking version of King Kong, only much larger. She'd complain about Blackie running loose, even though my dog always stayed on our property.

When my mom was ready to go, I walked out with her—just in time to see the masseuse calling Blackie into her house. My mom was furious and went next door to get my dog back. She asked nicely at first, but the Swedish woman blew her off, and a few minutes later a guy from the dog pound came around. Our neighbor had dropped the dime on Blackie!

Since my dog had no tags, the guy couldn't release him to my mom; we'd have to go down to the pound later and retrieve him. I didn't know what they did at the pound, but I figured it was some kind of jail for dogs. My mom was so upset that it had to be something terrible.

My mother went straight back up on our neighbor's porch and said, "If you ever do that to me again, Mrs. Bawl, I'm going to beat the hell out of you!"

"You're going to do *what?*" the Swedish woman said and shoved my mom, who fell down four cement steps, scraping her back along the way. My mother—my skinny little *mother!*—got back up and grabbed this bitch by her hair and started swinging her around like they do in wrestling matches. It was quite a sight—my mom was so frail looking, and she wasn't a brawler at all, but she had this huge masseuse by the head and was kicking the shit out of her. She was literally swinging this Hulk Hogan lookalike around the yard by her hair.

"Go get her, Blondie!" yelled a man from across the street. The guy from the pound just stood there with his mouth hanging open. And I remember thinking, *This is great!* I'd never seen my mom act so fierce before. My mom was so *cool*. (I didn't use the word "cool" at the time, of course, but I knew it when I saw it, even at four.)

When my mom finally ran out of steam, the masseuse was left on her knees, defeated and humiliated in front of the entire neighborhood. The one thing that ruined my mother's "Rocky" moment was the fact that she was late for the theater. She was also a mess, her face was sweaty and her makeup was running down her cheeks. As she rushed to the car, her Marie Antoinette curls flopping in her face, I remember thinking, *Boy, Mom, I have a completely new respect for you.*

And Nurse Ratched never bothered any of us again.

My First Television Epiphany

My grandparents—we called them Mamaw and Pa— were the first ones to get a television. We would all sit together and watch boxing, baseball, Milton Berle. Boxers bored me—mostly I remember the Texaco commercial. A whole bunch of men in uniforms running around a gas station singing, "We are the men from Texaco, we serve from Maine to Mexico." One day there was no such thing as television, and the next day you had these little people running around inside this box. Amazing.

When I was five, we got our own television, a maple console with a bigger screen than Mamaw and Pa's. Like everyone else in the house, I was so excited that I couldn't bear it, but *I* had to take a nap! The adrenaline was pumping through my little five-year-old veins, and there was no way I could sleep. I closed my eyes and pretended, but then my father came in and said, "I know you're not sleeping. C'mon, get up!"

I walked into the living room, where the grown-ups were sitting, and that's when I saw *One Million B.C.* Reality was suspended. I became one with the prehistoric cast, completely absorbed, I just meshed into the screen with them. I fell out-of-my-mind in love with Victor Mature (what a hunk). That movie was all I could think about for days.

My affinity for film was unnatural, even then.

My First Memory of (Being Dark) in Darkest Mexico

A trip down to Ensenada with my mother and her friends was a big deal. We'd stay in a cheap hotel on the beach, and there were always lots of kids around to play with. A real holiday.

But I hated passing through Tijuana to get there. You'd see broken-down houses, and people drinking out of dirty washbasins—there was so much poverty, so blatant and in your face. Tijuana was Africa-poor. I felt powerless and awful. It just wrecked me.

"Why doesn't somebody do something about this?" I asked my mother, a routine question for me. My mom was very much into helping people, one-on-one, even though we had almost nothing ourselves, but I never liked her answer. "This is just the way things are sometimes, Cher." Or, "It's such a big problem . . ." All those stupid things grown-ups say when they can't figure out what to do.

I also couldn't understand how tourists could stroll into the curio shops in Tijuana while people were out there starving on the streets, even children my age and younger. It got to the point where I'd just as soon close my eyes till we passed through that town.

I was maybe eight years old this one time when they stopped us at the border on our way back home. I always had a tan, and after three days in the sun and the ocean, I'd be black.

Me, stealing a gulp of beer from my mom and her best friend, Jake.

The border guards decided that I was Mexican, and that my mom was trying to smuggle me into America. They took us into their office and started asking me these silly questions that no little girl would know the answers to: "What's the name of the baseball team in St. Louis?" "What is the capital of North Dakota?" "What was Babe Ruth's mother's maiden name?"

Those idiot guards grilled us for about an hour. At first my mom was laughing, because it was so ridiculous, but then she got furious. I was getting pretty cranky my own damn self. I couldn't really understand why we were being harassed, but I figured that it had something to do with my looking different from my mother and little sister. They saw a dark person with two light people, and they weren't going for it.

Finally they let us pass. My perfect English sank in, I guess. Plus I think they were intimidated by my mother, who could be a force to be reckoned with once you set her off, and she was pretty pissed by now.

That day I learned that white/pale/blond/fair was *better*—or maybe just easier.

My dad—I always think of him that way (with Mom and me).

My First Memory of My Sister

One day my parents came back from the doctor's office with a surprise: My mom was pregnant. I didn't know what that meant, but the surprise was wonderful! We were going to get a baby from the *Baby Store* or from under a *cabbage leaf,* or the *Stork,* or the *Gypsies* . . . (No, the Gypsies stole you if you were bad.) Oh hell, one was just going to fall out of heaven! (What bullshit anyway.) I was so longing for a baby sister; it was all I could think about.

I remember being awakened in the middle of the night—it was *time!* I was taken to Mamaw's house while my mom went to the hospital. The first day she came home with my baby sister, Georganne, my mother was really nervous. My sister cried constantly, and nobody paid any attention to me at all. *The baby, the baby, the baby . . .*

I went into my little bedroom to take a nap, and my father came in and said, "I think I'll take a nap with you." We lay down, and he said, "You know, I don't know why everybody's making all the fuss. I don't think much of this new baby. What do you think?"

"I don't know," I said. "I didn't get to see her that much—everybody's always running around her."

"I know," my father said. "Let's go in and kidnap her."

So we got up and took my sister out of her bassinet and brought her back onto my bed. She was making little scriggy faces and looking around. "You know, she doesn't really do anything," my father said. "But we'd better keep her till she grows some hair!" (That wound up taking years, but we got attached to her while we were waiting.)

My father was really smart about things like that. I loved him, more than he could ever know. ⌒◦

My First Memories of My Grandparents

When my mother was at work, I usually stayed with one of my grandmothers, either Grandma Lynda or Mamaw.

GRANDMA LYNDA AND
GRANDPA CHARLIE

Grandma Lynda, my mother's mother, would sometimes get embarrassed by my Grandpa Charlie, who was a sweet man but absolutely unsophisticated. Grandpa Charlie had grown up with twelve brothers and sisters in a log cabin in Placerita Canyon, eighty miles or so outside Los Angeles, where all the Westerns were filmed. He developed recipes for the Johnson Pie Company, and sometimes he'd bring his work home. "If you can eat it all, it's all yours," he once told me, setting down a chocolate cream pie. I ate the whole thing in one sitting and have never tasted anything like it since.

Grandpa Charlie's father, who I called Papa Walker, still lived by himself in the cabin he'd built. He'd bought an expensive trailer, but he didn't like staying there, so he stored feed in it. Papa was a burly, red-cheeked outdoorsman who wore flannel shirts and one-piece long johns underneath. He'd feed the local deer, and when I came to visit I would watch them through the window of the cabin, just a few feet away. My grandmother told me that the cabin was Santa's house, and that these were his reindeer.

One day I went out to Grandpa Charlie's backyard and saw one of my reindeer hung on a hook off a tree. My grandfather had grown up hunting for venison, and he'd gotten a yen for some. I was just completely and utterly appalled. Grandma Lynda tried to explain it to me, but I wasn't going for any of that "Now, Cher, all deer aren't Bambi" crap.

My Grandma Lynda; she was only thirty-two in this picture. She's beautiful, isn't she, like a Gypsy. I'm on my way to a Porky Pig lookalike contest.

MAMAW AND PA

Mamaw was one of those mercurial Texans, like the little girl with the curl. She had a temper that she'd lose all the time with Pa, my grandfather, and then she'd be just fine. But she hardly ever lost her temper with me; she was wonderful with me and my sister, Georganne. Once she bought a broomstick and some clothesline rope and made me a trapeze in the backyard, hung off the limb of her lemon tree. In her sewing room she had a big tin button box, and I'd sit and play with it for hours on end, under her sewing machine. That box started my love affair with shiny things.

Pa was the smartest man I ever knew, and the laziest. You could ask him about anything, and he'd know the answer, he was like a walking—well, maybe a sitting—encyclopedia. "Well, darlin' . . . ," he'd start, and then he'd tell you much more than you ever wanted to know about the question you'd just asked him, and a lot more than you could comprehend. When he was a young man, he invented a traffic light, using a

*Mamaw and Pa. They were so
influential in my little life.
Aren't they cute?*

vacuum-cleaner motor, an alarm clock, and red and green lightbulbs. He sold it for $75,000 back in Texas. Now he liked to sit in front of the television in a big stuffed chair and drink iced tea (with lemon—ugh!) and watch every baseball game that was playing in the universe.

I was at their house one afternoon when he asked Mamaw to sew a piece of suede into an oblong pouch and fill it with dried beans. At first I thought she was making me moccasins, but then my grandfather took the suede pouch out to the garage (where he liked to tinker). When he came back in from the garage, he was carrying the pouch in his hand. He had put a tiny wire and two knobs into it. He ran the tiny wire from the pouch under the carpet to the back of the television. He placed the beanbag pouch on the arm of his overstuffed chair and then manipulated the dials in the pouch. I was amazed!

He could change the channel and turn the volume up and down without touching the television. Pa had invented a remote control! He never sold it, though—he was just doing it for himself because he was too lazy to get up from that old stuffed chair.

The First (of Many, Many) Times My Sister Got Me in Trouble

Once Georganne wasn't so new anymore, everything settled down. I'd been pining for a Tiny Tears doll, but a real live sister was even better. "You have to help take care of the baby," my mom told me, "because now you're the big one, and I need your help." And from the time she was three months old, I had to watch my baby sister.

Georganne was cute and blond, always laughing and giggling, and I had so much fun playing with her. But we still had the occasional catastrophe. Once I brought a bunch of my toys into the playpen for us, never thinking that she would wind up swallowing the tiny rubber wheels off my best blue car. When they found out, my mom was hysterical, and my dad was just pissed. I got sent to my room, but it was so over my head. (The baby did *what?* And *I was to blame for it?*)

They called the doctor, and for the next couple of days they had to poke through my sister's diapers with a Popsicle stick, until they found the last damn wheel. It was rough going for me for a while. But it was just a *small* example of things to come. ⟿

My First Protest / Walkout

When I was in fourth grade, we had what was called a "sharing day" at my school. The other kids all brought in their favorite toy or flowers from their garden, or they talked about what they did in the summertime, or they read a poem.

I was going to share something nice, too, but as one little kid after another got up and told some boring-ass story, it got to be too much for me. I couldn't bear all the *Leave It to Beaver* crap. When I got up to the front of the room to share, this is what I shared: "You guys are stupid, this school is stupid, and this sharing bullshit is stupid, so I'm going home." And I walked home, in the middle of the school day.

When my grandmother asked me why I was home so early, I told her, and she fell on her ass, laughing. When my mom heard about it, she fell on her ass, too.

My family rewarded that kind of independent behavior; they loved an individualist. Boy, if they'd only known what was ahead of them.

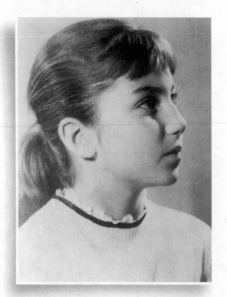

Who would think that this sweet child would grow up to be "Cher"?

The First Time I Realized That "Love Hurts"

People drank pretty freely in my parents' crowd, but it affected my father (technically, my stepfather) differently from everyone else. At first he'd be having a great time, and then he would go one drink too far. He'd stop laughing. He'd get belligerent and argumentative—he wasn't the same person at all. You'd just have to sit there and agree with everything he said and try to slip out of the room while he wasn't looking, if you could.

My mother hated it when my father drank, because it threw everything into turmoil. Once she told me that he'd gotten jealous at a big party and dragged her across the floor. When they started arguing at home, I'd get sent to my room, but I could still hear the violent yelling. I just tried to be quiet and invisible in my bed. I hated those fights; they made me a nervous wreck at four.

I knew my mother and father were crazy about each other, but they also tortured each other. They were young, jealous and immature; kind of like Sean and Madonna. They'd separate for months and then go back to each other. They split up for good when I was nine. I was so sad about it and missed my dad, but I knew we were better off without him. I'd already gotten the idea from my mom that men were these things that you loved against your will.

He still visited my sister and me from time to time. But then he got a new wife named Jane and moved back to Texas. We didn't see him much after that.

The strange thing is that I'm still very close to Jane.

My First Ticket to Ride

In my gang, I was the ringleader. I was always the one who'd say, "Let's go to the park." Or, "Let's put on a show." Or, "Let's go to Hornsby's Liquor Store," which was actually the convenience store where they'd give you a free ice cream, and a Coke in one of those old green bottles, on your birthday.

I was also the only kid without a bicycle, but it never stopped me. I'd either borrow a bike or ride on someone's handlebars. But by the time I was eight years old, a bicycle was all I thought about. I wanted it more than anything; I also knew we couldn't afford it. We were so broke that Georganne and I had to stay at Mamaw's for six months while my mom lived in a rented garage apartment with an eight-dollar-a-month fold-up bed.

On the day of my ninth birthday party, I was standing on my grandmother's porch, in my two-piece pink-and-white seersucker bathing suit, when my mom pulled up to the curb. At first she was blocked by the slope of the lawn, and I couldn't see what she was taking out of the car. Then I saw it, and my mouth dropped open. I was in total shock.

I walked down to the most beautiful bicycle I'd ever seen in my life, and gaped at it—I couldn't believe it was really mine. It was maroon with gold pinstriping, and it had three speeds and narrow racing tires. It was the kind I'd only seen in magazines, much nicer than any of my friends' bikes.

My mom told me later that she'd gotten it wholesale from a friend who owned an appliance store.

I got on that bike in my bathing suit, and left my party; I didn't come back till after sunset. I just kept going and going and going. It was the first time I felt free.

My First Run-In with the Yuban Can

My mother was fabulous in a crisis, though after it was taken care of, she'd completely fall apart. When I was nine years old, I used to climb to the top of my swing set and then do flips off of it onto the ground. My sister kept her Crayolas in an old coffee can, and one day while she was coloring under the swings, I did a flip and came down on the coffee can. I was barefoot, and landed on the edge of the can with my full weight. My foot was just hanging there, and my toes were all backwards and they wouldn't do anything. I saw blood everywhere and started screaming—I must have been in shock. I knew it was bad, but I wasn't sure exactly what had happened.

My mother ran from the house out to the backyard. She happened to have some dish towels in her hands. She wrapped my foot in the dish towels real tightly, and rushed me to the emergency room. The receptionist wanted her to fill out some forms, but my mom started yelling that she wanted me to see the doctor *now*. It was a *Terms of Endearment* kind of deal.

The nurses laid me down on the table, and when the doctor (actually he was an intern) went, "Oh God!" I got really scared. I had cut my foot to the bone. The tendons were severed and had snapped all the way back to my knee joint, like rubber bands. They had to take these long hooks and go up underneath my skin to bring them back down so they could be sewn together again. When my mom saw that, she just fell to her knees on the floor. I was in a cast for the rest of the summer.

Upon a follow-up visit, my regular doctor (who'd been on vacation when the accident happened) saw it and told my mother that the intern had sewn it up wrong and that I might never have the complete use of my foot. She was devastated, but told me that everything was fine. I did hobble around for quite some time after they took the cast off. However, in the end, my love of dancing was powerful enough to overcome my wanky left foot! ～◯

My First Time on the Mood Swing

The way I saw it, my mother was a goddess, sometimes a cranky one, but a goddess nonetheless. She seemed at least six feet tall (in reality, more like five-seven), and weighed in at about 25 pounds, soaking wet. She had beautiful blond hair that hung almost to her waist, and a terrific sense of humor. (I was a connoisseur of talent, even then.) She also carried what I know now to be the family gift, also its curse.

My mom had a temper, and no patience at all if you broke or ruined something. Once she got me a brand-new quilted robe, white with little blue flowers and round blue buttons, and a matching nightgown. I dropped a cup of hot tea all over myself—good-bye robe—and my mother went ballistic. Of course I was crying, because it was the nicest robe and nightgown I'd ever had. It was basically your lose-lose situation.

My mother was also a spanker. Once she told me that I couldn't walk a friend home, so I thought, *Okay, I'll just walk her to the corner.* When I came back to my house, I remember seeing my mom in the doorway. Her voice was really hoarse from tonsillitis, and she'd been calling me. I got the mother of all spankings.

I would never talk back to my mother, but she sensed early on that I was basically uncontrollable. You just look at your child and you *know.* I had always been considered a moody child. My family loved me, but I was kind of an enigma, even as a little kidlet. Imagine me running around your house, a tiny Cher-in-waiting. I know my mother loved me dearly, but I also think I scared the shit out of me.

On days that my mom was feeling good, she'd sing and talk and play around and have a great time. But on her not so good days, she'd be quiet and down. She'd make us dinner then go to bed early. She didn't like to watch TV alone so she'd say, "Girls, do you want to make popcorn and watch TV in my bed?"

While I worried about these spells, I knew that my mother worked hard taking care of me and Gee, and sometimes she just ran out of gas. So I accepted them as part of who she was. She was different from other mothers—she had this great, lively side to her, and then there was the other side. She could walk out of a room happy and come back in melancholy. When you're small, it's hard to figure out what's going on with grown-ups.

Sometimes I thought she was just being arbitrary, and it drove me crazy. But then there were moments when I saw that she had to gather herself together one minute at a time. ⟶

No matter what our financial situation was, my mom tried to get Christmas together in a major way.

My First House

When I was nine, we moved from a horrible apartment to a little two-bedroom rented house in the San Fernando Valley. It was the homiest place we'd ever ever lived in (excluding my grandparents' homes).

The house was made of redwood, with white trim around the windows and doors. Inside it was like a mountain cabin, all knotty pine, with beamed ceilings. My sister and I shared a room that my mom had wallpapered herself. It was a pretty powder-blue wallpaper with butterflies. She could do almost everything around the house; she even put on a new roof once!

My mom loved living on Beeman Avenue. All our neighbors were great to her, plus her best friend, Jake, lived next door. My sister and I loved it, too. There were millions of kids to play with and big backyards to play in. All of us kids ran around like wild banshees; it was a child's paradise.

I like this picture of me and Gee. It's my cheery face. Actually it's my father's face—I'm just borrowing it! My mom called this our squeaky clean look. It was a Saturday/Sunday kind of thing.

We had an apricot tree and a peach tree out front, and on our birthdays my mom would hang suckers from one and balloons from the other. In the summertime, all the kids from the neighborhood would come over at night and sit on quilts while my mom told ghost stories.

We didn't need much to entertain us. One of my favorite memories of that house and my friends was one summer when we sneaked into the vacant lot next door to play logrollers on empty water drums, which were about four feet high. Four of us at a time would take turns standing on the huge drums and rolling them all over the lot with our feet. That thrilled us all for an entire summer.

Three houses on our block shared an old brick barbecue and a badminton court. We'd set up our Fourth of July firecrackers on the court and then stay up late and eat barbecued chicken, corn on the cob, and coleslaw. The only downside to all this gaiety was that you could burn your feet on used sparklers (of course, I was always running around barefoot). ⌒๑

My First Food Flirtation

My mom was born in Arkansas and grew up in Oklahoma, and she was a real Southern cook: collard greens, fried chicken, corn bread. Great vegetable plates, with mashed potatoes and black-eyed peas and corn on the cob. We had watermelon and cantaloupe, and a big pitcher of iced tea was always on the kitchen table. The one thing we did without was steak. Come to think of it, red meat in general.

When I was small, my mom shopped in the only health food store in the Valley. We had dried fruits and raw nuts to snack on. But she also made fudge, popcorn and chocolate chip cookies with us. My mom was a walking dichotomy.

On very special occasions, we'd get to go out to an inexpensive restaurant. My mom loved Dupar's, which she said was like a poor man's Chasen's. I'd always order fried shrimp: I thought that was the best thing in the world.

The chain restaurants weren't a big deal in those days. There was a Bob's Big Boy in the Valley, and *a* McDonald's, where I'd stop on the way home from school. It was the first McDonald's. It had golden arches out front, and a sign that said something like, 28,000 SOLD. Mr. McDonald (actually I believe his name was Kroc) worked behind the counter and made our hamburgers by hand and chocolate malts with real ice cream. It was nothing like fast food today (which is total crap and will kill you).

I can remember a few times, though, when we went hungry. Once we had stew for a week, and I swore I would never eat it again. At our lowest point, we had nothing but soda crackers. One time I got so angry, because there were ants in the soda crackers, and I just thought, This is too much to bear! (I was so Scarlett O'Hara . . .)

Whenever we had some extra money, we would get something from the Helms Bakery Man. He came around with his van twice a week. He'd sound his funny ship's whistle, and the kids in the neighborhood would all go running to the back of the van. He'd pull out these huge drawers, which contained all of my dream foods: fresh donuts and cakes and the most incredible chopped walnut squares, sixty cents for an eight-by-ten-inch tin. That was my first experience with powdered sugar; it was magic; it disappeared in your mouth.

I was crazy about the Helm's Bakery Man. I wanted to marry him when I grew up, probably just to get free bakery goods . . . I wonder if he felt used. ⟶

My First Broadway Fantasy

When I was three, I used to run around the house naked, singing. (I bet that comes as a shock!) I could hear a song once and remember every word. I think I was five when we went to see *Cinderella.* On the way home, I sat in the backseat and sang "A Dream Is a Wish Your Heart Makes." My mother was dumbstruck. "Are you hearing what she's doing?" she said to my father. "Do you *hear* this child?"

My mom loved to buy the cast albums of hit Broadway musicals. *Porgy and Bess, My Fair Lady, Oklahoma!*—they were all great, but my favorite was *West Side Story.* The others were period pieces, with older characters, but *West Side Story* was about young people in a modern setting; I could relate to it. I'd never been to New York, and the movie version didn't come out till years later, but I could look at the album cover and visualize the rest.

I was shy but I loved to put on shows for my mother and sister. Except for *West Side Story;* that one was always private for me. I'd wait till nobody else was home, and then I'd turn up the volume on the record player full blast, and I'd dance around the living room singing all the parts. I identified with every character, not just the women. It takes a long time to learn a whole cast album, and I kept working on that musical for months. I never showed it to anyone, not even my mom. Years later, I played all the parts of *West Side Story* in a TV special I did. (Those months all alone in my living room really paid off.)

The First Time I Realized That I Wouldn't Be Going to Bryn Mawr

When I was young, I went to a million different schools. I kept falling further and further behind in my schoolwork because of it. My spelling was terrible; I couldn't read quickly enough to get all my homework done, and for me, math was like trying to understand Sanskrit. It was embarrassing for me not to be able to do the schoolwork that everyone else was doing. Was I stupid? I didn't think I was. But all the signs pointed in that direction. I didn't like authority, and I couldn't understand the lessons. School was a bitch for me. The only way I learned was by listening to my teachers in the classroom.

My mother never talked about my going to college. "You're so great at other things," she would tell me. "You can sing, and you're funny and artistic." She'd say, "There's nothing you can't accomplish if you put your mind to it." And I believed her. My sister was the brain; I was the weird one, the artist.

Of course, I had the kind of mom who thought nothing about packing her daughters off to the drive-in theater on a school night. The next day I'd sit in class and daydream about the movies we'd seen the night before and relive them, with myself as the leading woman, man or dog—I was an equal-opportunity daydreamer.

Or I'd think about what I'd be when I grew up. When I was really little I thought I was an angel sent by God to find the cure for polio and save the world. You can't imagine how pissed off I was when Jonas Salk beat me to the punch.

My First Public Performance

At the end of fifth grade, I put on <u>Oklahoma!</u> almost single-handedly. I got four or five girls together, but I did the direction and choreography, and I played all the boys' parts (in grammar school you just can't get boys to do anything that's the least bit risky . . . what am I talking about, grammar school). I sang the Gordon MacRae songs (my voice was low, even then) plus "Poor Judd Is Dead" and "Everything's Up to Date in Kansas City."

We performed for our class and teacher, and it was the last thing on the last day before the bell rang for summer vacation! There was so much electricity. Summer was starting . . . everything was possible. As we got ready to go on, I felt a weird combination of nervousness and excitement—maybe more nervousness at that point.

I remember that the boys in our audience were dumbstruck. I don't think they knew what a play was, much less a musical. This one boy was staring at me with his head cocked, as if to say, *What are you doing? What are we watching?* He looked at me like the R.C.A. dog. (I realize how this dates me! Oh well.) By the end, though, they got swept up into the sheer spectacle of it all.

As they cheered, I was thinking: *Well, it wasn't perfect.* It was a very hit-and-miss production. One of the numbers just hadn't worked. *If we'd only had costumes, if we'd had more people in the cast, and more time to rehearse. . . .* I was like a pint-size Bob Fosse. Take a chill pill, Cher, you've got your whole life to be tense.

My First Utter Humiliation

I was about to finish fourth grade, and I knew that everyone would dress up for the last day of school, but times were tough at our house. The day before, my mother presented me with new shoes: the ugliest pair of tan and brown open-toe boy-looking sandals I had ever seen. I thought, *How can I go to school in them?*

I was already feeling embarrassed about having to make do with my old pink pinafore dress. My mom was upset that I was upset, mostly because it was all she could afford. She'd only had four dollars in the world, and girls' dress shoes cost seven or eight dollars then.

I felt traumatized at school the next day. Everyone else had these cute little Mary Janes, white ones or black ones, which made what I had on look even bulkier and more hideous, especially next to my pink socks. Oh my God, I hated those sandals so much! It seemed impossible to me that my mother couldn't have found something better; I would have rather worn the fucking shoe box!

"Oh, you decided not to dress up," somebody said to me.

"Yeah," I muttered, wanting to fall through the floor. Even the poorest girl in the school, the one whose hair was always messy, had a white nylon dress with little flowers on it and matching shoes that day. Even the poorest girl looked better than me.

My First Taste of La Dolce Vita

My mother always wanted a rich husband, but she always fell in love with poor men.

Except for this one time at a party at Doris Duke's house when she met a millionaire builder named Joseph Harper Collins. He asked my mom to marry him fifteen minutes after they met. She said yes two weeks later; she was bowled over by him, she said. (He must have been one helluva bowler.)

So we moved from our teeny redwood house on Beeman Avenue to a mansion in Beverly Hills. There was a swimming pool, a cook, a housekeeper and a butler named Big John who was fabulous. He had a wooden leg, and sometimes he'd let me and Georganne play soldier with it.

Joe Collins was a big guy all around, totally larger than life. I thought he was nuts, but he was great with me and my sister, so lively, so much fun—I think we got along with him much better than Mom did. Whatever we wanted to do was fine with him, as long as we didn't go into the wing where his mother lived. She was sick, with oxygen and all that kind of stuff.

Everything was changed. Now I went on a school bus with Tina Sinatra. (She used to sit by herself with her hair pulled back in a little bun; she was so beautiful, I couldn't take my eyes off her.) I ate real steak for the first time, and lobster became my favorite food. My mom got a pink Cadillac convertible; she bought beautiful clothes, lots of fox-trimmed things. Life seemed a lot less stressful for her and therefore for me too. Her friends had never been exposed to such opulence; they were delighted to come over to the house for parties and barbecues; they all oohed and aahed. I got a kick out of them.

The marriage lasted five months. We moved back to the Valley (oh, God, how I hate the Valley), first to a bigger house than the one we left on Beeman Avenue, then all the way back to our little redwood box. I didn't want to go, but I got over it. I knew that the mansion in Beverly Hills was only a dream. It was just a lovely fantasy.

The First Time I Saw the King

In 1957 I started to become aware of rock 'n' roll.
I think the first actual record I bought was "Tequila," by the Champs.
I can remember running home from school and turning on *American Bandstand.* Ray Charles was playing the piano and singing "Georgia on My Mind." I cried. I thought it was the greatest thing I'd ever heard. This music was special to me in a way that was impossible for me to explain to anyone. It was like the movie *Rebel Without a Cause.* It expressed how it felt to be a teenager, and when I saw Elvis on *The Ed Sullivan Show,* I was a goner. I loved the way he sang and the way he looked. In some strange way, I felt he expressed who I was.

I got into rock 'n' roll a little bit early because my mom loved it, too. She thought the music was actually good, and she wasn't threatened by it like most of my friends' mothers were. When I was eleven, Mom took me to see Elvis at the Pan-Pacific Auditorium. He was wearing a gold suit and was truly cool, but the thing that made the biggest impression on me was seeing all the teenage girls screaming and jumping up and down on their chairs.

"Why are they doing that?" I asked my mother.

"You'll find out in a little while," she said.

"Can we stand up on our chairs and jump up and down and scream, too, Mom?"

"Sure," she said, and we did.

The First Time I Met My Father

My mother never talked about John Sarkisian and neither did anyone else in the family. Somewhere in my young consciousness, I had a vague idea about some strange father out in the universe, but it was more a feeling than information. Since no one ever talked about him, I figured the subject was closed. It never really bothered me because I was so crazy about my stepfather.

One night, when I was eleven years old, my mother asked me out of nowhere, "Would you like to meet your father?"

"Sure," I said in a casual way, like we'd talked about him a million times. I didn't feel a burning desire to meet him; however, I was curious, and I must have been a little bit excited, too.

The next day I put on my good dress; my mother stuck curlers in my hair and sat me under her big metal dryer that seemed to burn my ears off. At some point that afternoon the doorbell rang, and I went to the door. I was nervous and when I opened the door my first thought was . . . *Whoa, that's my smile.* (My mom used to look at me strangely when I made a certain kind of smile. Now, I suddenly realized why.)

My father was Armenian. He was about two inches taller than my mother, and well built. He seemed strong. He had curly black hair and dark, slanty eyes like mine and big fluffy eyebrows. He looked a lot like me, and I thought once again . . . *Now I understand. This is where I come from.* I knew then why I looked the way I looked, that I hadn't been brought here by Gypsies who hid me under a cabbage leaf. (Oh Mom, you are such a kidder!)

My mom would always get furious with me because I ate so slowly. She thought I was dawdling, but it was just my pace. At dinner that night, I saw that my father ate slowly, too. I was thrilled.

My father was extremely well dressed, and what I was particularly struck by was his beautiful alligator shoes. I had never seen anything like them before. I asked him if they were expensive. When he said they cost eighty-five dollars, it floored me. I would never have believed that men spent that kind of money on clothes. (It took me forever to save up for my roller skates, and they only cost twenty-one dollars and were my prize possession.)

My father seemed nice; he was fun to be around; however, I remember feeling a little bit standoffish. There was something that kept me from buying the whole package. I really did want to like him, but he was a stranger. He was just a man who'd walked into our house with my smile.

My mom and my real dad—he was a sweet man, but a stranger to me.

My First Decision to Become Famous

Whenever I was feeling defeated or excluded, my mother would say, "If it doesn't matter in five years, it doesn't matter." If I was heartbroken, she would tell me, "You might not be the prettiest or the most talented, you might not be the smartest, but you're special." I got that locked into my brain and I never forgot it.

Though for a long time I felt more *different* than special, and different is not good when you're young. I was popular, but I was weird, too. The kids liked me in spite of the fact that I'd go to a movie and root for the villain, or that I longed to be a beatnik and wear black.

But my mother always thought that I'd do something special. I didn't want to be a nurse or a doctor or a housewife or a teacher. It was show business for me, from as early as I can remember, though I wasn't sure how it would happen. I doubted that I could be an actress, and none of the big-name singers looked like me. They looked like Connie Stevens or Doris Day. *That's what I'd like to do,* I thought, but I wasn't sure if people who didn't look all-American ever got a chance to do it.

So I decided I just wanted to be famous—maybe not with a specific talent, like Judy Garland or Dorothy McGuire, but as a *personality.* Like Merv Griffin or Dinah Shore. Television seemed like a place where you could be famous just by being friendly.

By age eleven, I was practicing my autograph. By the time I was twelve, I had it down (basically the same as I sign it now). I did it over and over again, because I was sure that one day I would need it.

It was always "Cher"; I never thought of myself as anything but "Cher." I went by different last names as a child, but none of them seemed really me. And no one ever called me by my real first name, Cherilyn, except maybe some teacher who wasn't close to me, or my mother when she was really pissed off.

Halloween was my favorite holiday,
needless to say.

My First Driving Experience

I was always a handful for my mother. Once I decided to run away from home with a friend of mine. We found a horse in a pasture and we took it. We rode the horse along the railroad tracks as far as we could (which was quite a ways). Then we let it go and jumped into a slow-moving boxcar. (What was I . . . preparing for—*Of Mice and Men?*) It was getting dark by the time we reached San Bernardino, and my friend got afraid and got off to call her mother. I got off, too, but I didn't really want to. I was having fun; I wanted to see how far I could go.

Around this time my grandfather Pa taught me to drive, and I loved it. I went from my bicycle obsession straight to cars. After a long series of crummy old Chevrolets and Studebakers, my mom got a red Pontiac convertible. On workdays she'd share a ride to the studio with a friend, leaving her car keys in the house to tempt me. They'd be calling out to me . . . "Cher, come and pick us up and take us into Hollywood." This was the beginning of my life as a car-napper.

One school day, when I was thirteen, I convinced my little sister to ride with me into Hollywood. Gee was game, as usual. She didn't know I wasn't supposed to be driving—well, she might have suspected, but she wasn't positive. It's a long way from Toluca Lake to Hollywood. I must have been nuts; I can't imagine what I was thinking.

Once we got started, I was nervous, but I wasn't about to turn back. *Don't run any red lights,* I told myself. *Stay on the road.* I was always tall, so I had no trouble reaching the pedals, and soon we'd reached our favorite hot dog stand on Hollywood Boulevard. After we ate our hot dogs, I headed back home.

The trip home was a little dodgier. I ran two red lights in front of the Hollywood Bowl, and at one point I banged into some garbage cans in an alleyway. "Oh boy," Gee said, "are you going to get in trouble if Mom finds out!"

Another one of my out-of-body driving experiences was when my best friend Della and I took my mother's Pontiac out for a spin. When we came back and pulled up in front of the house, we saw my mother on the lawn; she had come home before us. I almost passed out—I thought it was the end of life as I knew it. I had stolen my mom's car, and I was sure that she would either kill me or put me in my room till I was forty and shove soda crackers under my door (ants and all). But I must have done something good in another life because a miracle happened; my mom had gotten distracted by something. She never saw Della and me pull up! I mean, what are the odds on that one? First you steal your mom's car; she comes home before you, and doesn't even notice that her car isn't parked where she left it. Then she's standing out on the front lawn as you and your girlfriend drive up in her *red* convertible that you have been out joyriding in. *There is a God.*

My First Bra

By the time I turned twelve, I was sure I needed a bra.
Of course I had nothing to put in a bra. But my mom was a pal and
said I could get one.

We went out to a department store in the Valley called The May
Co. I was so excited. My first bra! It was really a glorified undershirt. A
flat little thing with some lacy bits and a couple of puckers on it. The
one I really wanted had slightly thicker material to give the appearance
that you had a bit more inside it but my mom said it didn't look good
on me. I only wore a size 32, 30, or maybe a 28 AAA—but I was out of
my mind with excitement. It was a huge milestone for me. I was on my
way to becoming "Annette" from the Mouseketeers.

While I was in the dressing room trying on my new bra, my mother
asked the saleswoman to come in. I felt naked, mortified. My mom
was poking at me, going, "Well, do you think it's a good fit? Do you
think the straps are right?" Had my mother suddenly lost what she
laughingly called her mind?

The saleswoman said, "Yes, I think it's a lovely fit. I wouldn't make
the straps any higher, you don't want it hiking up in the back." And
then this stranger was touching me, pushing and pulling my new bra.

I couldn't move. I was catatonic. I wanted to disappear into China.
I was humiliated. Oh, Mother; Mother, how could you? How can I
ever hold my head up high again? How will I ever be able to trust you
again, *Mother!*

We bought two bras, so I could wash one and wear one. I was so
happy I could have danced home wearing my two new bras hooked together to form a stole. But I had to keep a kind of a low profile in front
of you-know-who. She might decide to invite strangers along the road-
side to join in the festivities.

My First Kiss
—or—
Head for the Roundhouse, Nellie. He Can't Corner You There

My first crush was on a boy named Milton Broadlight. We were both in the fifth grade, in the same overcrowded classroom, but he was in five A and I was in five B, so we never sat together. Milton Broadlight had black, black hair and blue, blue eyes and long black eyelashes. I mooned over him from across the room with that dying-calf-in-a-thunderstorm look. But it wasn't working out. He thought I was just a kid.

I did, however, have my first date at the end of that year. My mom had a friend with an older son, maybe thirteen, and he needed a date for a hayride. I had never gone anywhere with a boy before—and now my mother was letting me go out at nighttime! The whole deal was pretty exciting.

We went out to the country in one of those old trucks with slatted wooden sides, filled with matted hay. I thought it would have been a lot better in an old wagon drawn by horses and with fresh hay, but it was a blast anyway.

At the end of the ride, the boy kissed me. I don't know exactly how it happened. The only time I'd seen kissing was on TV, or with my aunt and uncle. (They were always kissing in front of me and sticking their tongues in each other's mouths—Ugh!)

But my first kiss wasn't awful at all. It made my head go all dizzy and floaty. And even though I didn't care that much for the boy, there was something about the kiss that I liked a lot. Yes, kissing was definitely in my future!

My First Religious Experience
—or—
None from None Is Nun

By the time I was ready to start junior high, I was falling in love every other minute. So my father decided I was just the right candidate for Catholic school. He paid the tuition and my mom packed me off to a Catholic boarding school in Burbank.

It was very hard for me in the beginning. Everything was different, strange. I wasn't a Catholic. I'd never been to Mass. There were a million ridiculous rules abou;everything: don't do this, don't say that, and it was lonely for me in the big dormitory, away from my mother and sister, and I hated getting up in the dark every morning to go to six o'clock Mass. I'd brought shorts and jeans for after school, but the nuns said I couldn't wear them. So I had to end up wearing a pink dress that I'd brought every day; by the end of the week, my name was "Pinky." That's what I was called the whole time I was there, "Pinky Sarkisian."

I made three really good friends at Villa Cabrini—Donna Payne, Rose Delurgeo, and Anita Fernandez—and soon I had a *pachuco* hairdo like theirs. Everyone wore their hair that way—it was just the thing to do.

And boy, oh boy, I heard stories there that would curl your hair, because the girls in Catholic school were the wildest girls I'd ever met. When we'd come back from our weekends at home, they'd tell about sneaking out to meet their boyfriends in the middle of the night. They were thirteen or fourteen years old and already having sex.

There was only one young man at Villa Cabrini. His name was Bruno. (He looked like Johnny Depp.) He was the Italian gardener's son. Bruno didn't speak a word of English, but that didn't stop him from getting laid more than any guy in the western hemisphere.

There were very strict rules for us to follow; one of them was "no makeup" whatsoever—they would check us out daily for blush-on and lipstick. However, the old nuns had bad eyesight, so they didn't realize that we were all lining our eyes with a black Maybelline eye pencil. I thought I looked so great until I came home one weekend and my mom stared at me and said, "Don't put that black crap around your eyes again, you look like a hooker."

Some of the sisters were mean, but the majority of them were fabulous. There was a young one who'd just come from Italy and looked like Sophia Loren. We loved her; however, nobody could understand why she'd joined the order. Although there was a time early on there when I thought about becoming a nun myself. I got so caught up in the architecture, the music, the candle lighting and the kneeling—the spectacle of the whole deal. But there were problems that I just couldn't overcome, like the history books where the Catholics were always the good guys. When I challenged something that I was sure wasn't true, it would cause no end of controversy. Our teacher, Sister Bernadette, who was Sheldon Leonard incarnate: Brooklyn accent and all; very funny; very cool; very tough. She'd say, "Pinky, can't you give me a break? Do we have to have these discussions every day? Why can't you wise up and keep your mouth shut?"

Our priest would come by every Friday to talk with us, and he and I would get into very heated discussions. Nobody else was even curious, but I'd say, "Do you mean to tell me, if a child dies and it's not baptized, it has to go to purgatory? What would a baby do that would be wrong? What sin could they possibly commit?"

The priest would explain, "We're sinful from the time we're born, Pinky. Why won't you take anything on faith?"

And I'd say, "I just don't see how it makes any sense." I liked the priest, but I didn't like those "because we say so" answers, and I really resented earning an "A" on my catechism test but being given a "B" because I wasn't baptized.

Then there was the time I was entertaining the dormitory after lights-out. My jokes weren't very original; however, the girls thought they were hilarious. I would also say funny things about our nuns (or what I thought were funny things) like, "Sister Theresa is so fat she waddles around the dining room like a duck." Or "Sister Josephine's teeth are like stars—they come out at night." Then for my pièce de résistance I said that Mother Benedetta (the mother superior) looked just like Joe E. Brown, the comedian with the amazing big mouth. (In fact, she looked *exactly* like him in *Some Like It Hot*.)

Just then the lights went on—it was Sister Josephine, and she'd heard every single thing. She was a big stoolie, and the next day I was sent to see Mother Benedetta. The mother superior was calm at first, until she said, "Pinky, these robes are sacred," and then a big hand came up out of nowhere and knocked me into next week.

After that, I had to say the rosary while walking across the grass—on my knees. Then I had to write five hundred times, "I will never say anything disparaging about the sisters again." Luckily, I was on the varsity volleyball team, and we had an important game coming up. So Sister Bernadette—the Sheldon Leonard nun—made everyone in class help me write out my penance so I could play in The Big Game.

My First Boyfriend . . .
— or —
Was It My First Fifteen Minutes of Fame?

When I was thirteen, I fell in love with the biggest jock at our school, a boy named Fred Smith. He was a big surfer who belonged to the posh group of rich kids in junior high. I, of course, was in the other group. He came up to me one day in the hash line, he was really nervous, and I couldn't believe he was talking to me, much less inviting me out on a date.

Fred was my first attempt at a boyfriend. We were crazy for each other for about fifteen minutes. Well, maybe I am stretching the longevity of our relationship by five minutes.

One night we went to a party with a group of kids, and all the boys were drinking, just to look cool. On the way back home, Fred started holding his head. When we got to my house, he staggered out of the car and puked all over my lawn. (I held his head; as far as I was concerned that was just part of the "love" experience.) I guess he was embarrassed after that, because he didn't talk to me for the longest time.

My First (and Only) Night in Jail

I was going on fourteen, and one night I went out with two girlfriends and one of their boyfriends; all of them were a few years older than me. The guy had a '57 Chevy (at that time it wasn't a big deal to have a '57 Chevy—it was just an old car). We drove over to the Kirkwood Bowling Alley in Studio City and pulled up near the front door. The boyfriend told us he needed to run in for a couple of minutes, but he didn't want to park the car. He asked me to sit behind the wheel since he had heard that I knew how to drive. He told me, "If someone should come up, just tell them to drive around you. I won't be very long."

We waited and waited but he didn't come back out, and my friends were getting kind of bored. After fifteen minutes, they started saying, "Let's go. You can drive, just do it." First we circled the parking lot, but he didn't come out. Then we went around the block, and he still wasn't there, so we decided to drive around for a little while. The boy had a bottle of vodka in the car, and we thought it would be very cool if we got some orange juice and made screwdrivers.

About three minutes after we pulled into a drive-in restaurant, before we could mix our first drink, the police arrived. My friend's boyfriend had reported the Chevy stolen. We got pulled out of the car, and all three of us immediately panicked. They didn't even need to give us the third degree; we told them everything by the second one. We were embarrassed, and also terrified that they'd find the vodka in the car and know what our orange juice was for.

They brought us in to a police station in the Valley. They were very nice policemen, but all I could think of was, *Oh my God, we're going to the Big House.* I was one of those people who went straight to the film version in any crisis. I could see myself with a number on my striped uniform, working all day in the prison laundry, and the lesbian guards cutting all my hair off . . . and killing a tiny little kitten who was my only friend . . . and then me losing my mind . . .

After we got to the station, we were put in separate holding rooms. The police were about to close the door to my room when I saw something moving under the bunk, and I shouted, "Wait a minute, don't leave!" It was some drunk, mumbling something about "I'll get that rotten bitch if it's the last thing I do." He was semiconscious, which was more conscious than I would have liked.

"Ah, shit," the policeman said. "We gotta put her someplace else."

It was after three in the morning when they finally reached my mom to come pick me up. She was surprisingly cool about the whole thing; I think she was too frightened to scream at me. The joyriding charges were dropped. I wasn't going to the Big House. "I hope you've learned your lesson," one of the policemen said. "You're too nice of a girl to be doing crazy things like this."

I never saw those two girlfriends again. Their mothers wouldn't let them talk to me. They said I was a bad influence. Oh, bullshit!

My First Sexual Experience
—or—
How Many Italians Does It Take to Screw in a Lightbulb?

By the time I was fourteen, my friends were doing everything but going all the way. They thought if you stopped short of the actual penetration part, you'd get some special dispensation. I thought they were totally full of shit. I wasn't doing anything, except kissing.

My latest mad passion was with my next-door neighbor, a short Italian guy named Jeff. He was a senior and four years older than me. He would work on his car every Saturday and Sunday, and I'd hand him the tools, and we'd talk about everything.

We got along perfectly—until his friends showed up. Then he'd start acting like I was this little kid who was always pestering him: "Okay, Cher, run on home now." But the minute his friends left, he'd be over at my house to watch a movie or listen to records. When we were alone, we'd have a great time together.

For a kid my age, Jeff was hard to understand. The other thing that bothered me was that he was always trying to talk me into having sex. We'd start kissing, and he'd keep pushing further and further, but I just wasn't going for it.

One night, Jeff came over and asked Mom if I could go to Bob's Big Boy with him to get a hamburger. My mom said it was okay, and I was thrilled. As we were getting ready to go, some of his friends dropped by and they teased him about hanging out with a girl my age. He didn't want them to know that he had asked me to go with him to dinner so he blew me off like some stupid kid.

I was hurt and furious (an extremely bad combination for me). I wouldn't talk to him the next day. I wouldn't even answer the door when he came over. About four days later, I finally let him in. We were sitting in my bedroom when I said, matter-of-factly, "You know that thing that you're always wanting to do? Well, let's do it."

Jeff looked at me like he'd just won the lottery. But he didn't waste any time. He wasn't exactly a master of foreplay so the sex was quick and painful. I kept thinking, *Is this what everyone's talking about?*

A few minutes later, as Jeff was putting his clothes on, I said, "Is that all there is . . . is that it?" (Oh! was I having a Peggy Lee moment.) When he said that it was, I told him, "Okay, you go home now, and don't ever come back to my house again." He looked shocked, and he left. I was kind of surprised at myself, but I wanted to hurt his feelings as badly as he'd hurt mine.

After he was gone, I ran to the mirror to look at my face because my mom had said that you could see it in a girl's face when she'd had sex. I thought, *Oh, my God, my mom's gonna come home from work and know. Everyone's gonna know.* I was afraid the words I HAVE JUST HAD SEX WITH THE BOY NEXT DOOR would be pulsating across my forehead in Day-Glo letters.

Jeff had lost a close friend, a person he could be himself with, and it really bothered him. He kept trying to come back over, but I wouldn't talk to him.

The next time my girlfriends were talking about boys, I broke in and said, "Oh yeah? Well, I did the real thing." They were stunned. "What's it like?" they all wanted to know.

I said, "If you guys like what you're doing, keep doing it; but don't go all the way."

My First New York Party

—or—

Big Apple Bites Cher

After my mother married Gilbert La Piere, we moved to New York. The city was bizarre and foreign, but thrilling to me. We arrived after Thanksgiving. It was the first time I'd been in cold weather, the first time I'd ever seen snow. I wanted to like New York right away, but I felt so isolated. I didn't know anybody, and since I wouldn't start school till after the holiday season, I wasn't going to meet anybody. I only went places with my mother and stepfather. I didn't understand how the city worked and I didn't have enough confidence to venture out into it by myself. I was just too shy.

By Christmas I was miserable; just moping around and crying all the time. The only guy I knew was our elevator operator, Jesse. He was a sweet guy, and when he invited me to a New Year's Eve party, I was thrilled. (I seem to have spent a lot of my teenage years being thrilled.) He promised my parents he'd take good care of me, and they liked him so much that they let me go.

The party was in a railroad flat down on Avenue C, in the East Village. I went in my nicest dress and high heels and my mom's fur coat— but I wasn't ready for what happened. I found myself in a scene right out of *West Side Story.* There were lots of strange-looking young guys in purple shirts and black ties, and girls with hair teased to death and piled a foot high on their heads, wearing primary-colored cha-cha-cha dresses, cracking their gum. While we were in the living room, a knife fight broke out in the kitchen. One of the guys came out with blood all over his shirt, and they had to rush him to the hospital. Happy New Year, Cher.

My First Subway Experience
—or—
How Would You Like to Take a Nice Ride in Hell, Cher?

New York was slow going for me socially until I met Joyce.
She was the daughter of one of my stepfather's business associates. Through Joyce I met Maxine and Barbara; they all lived on Riverside Drive. They were funny, and they all sounded like Joan Rivers to me; I was mesmerized. Their families seemed so warm, even though they yelled a lot, and their mothers were so motherly. Sometimes I even went to temple with them.

When summer came around we all decided to go to the beach. So this one Saturday, I threw on some jeans and a T-shirt over my bathing suit and took the subway with my friends out to Jones Beach. Halfway there, they got out of the train to check our directions, and the door shut before they could get back inside. I was on my own. Oh shit!

I had no idea where I was going. In that subway train, I went into sensory overload. I got so frightened that I couldn't even speak, much less ask someone for directions. I went all the way to the end of the line, just sitting and sweating, hoping that the train would bring me back to where I'd started.

As if all of this wasn't bad enough, the zipper of my jeans broke and I didn't know it. I sat for the longest time wondering why all these old men were smiling these smarmy smiles at me. Then I looked down and saw my jeans completely open. I was mortified! I started crying. Crying and sweating. Not a very attractive look, believe me.

Four hours after I'd started, I finally made my way back to River-side Drive and Barbara's house. Her mom hugged me after I fell through her doorway, a mess of tears and perspiration, sobbing hysterically. That was my first subway ride, and my last. ⟿

My First Role Model

My mother had blond hair and green eyes. My sister was a strawberry blonde. My Uncle Mickey was blond, like just about everyone on my mom's side. I was always the dark one. Dark hair, dark eyes, dark skin.

It wasn't just that blondes were the pretty ones. They were also the good ones. Women with black hair like mine were either evil queens or witches in all the Disney movies. In the real films they were always the ones who lost the man and got their just desserts in the end. They had black moods; black thoughts; they did black deeds and were prone to dark brooding moments in the shadows—there were so many ways to drive this concept home.

I knew I wasn't cute; I wasn't adorable and I wasn't all-American looking. "Someday," my mother said, "you're going to be happy that you look the way you look." But "someday" has no meaning when you're a teenager. I wanted to be a blonde. I pined to be a blonde. I wanted to trade in my cheekbones for a round face with blue eyes and a little pug nose. I wanted to look like Sandra Dee.

In 1961, *Breakfast at Tiffany's* came out, and Audrey Hepburn immediately became my idol. Not that we looked alike, but at least she wasn't blonde, and she was a little bit *irregular.* I rushed home from the movie theater and told my mom, "Oh, Mother, you've got to see this picture—I've just seen a girl who's exactly like me!"

From that day on I started dressing like Holly Golightly, with my hair in little pigtails. And I wore big sunglasses all the time; indoors and out, which broke the rules at Montclair, the school I went to. The principal called me to his office and said, "You know what, Cher? You're going to have to follow some rules." Then he suspended me for a week. (Well, Mr. Simpson. It wasn't in me or Holly Golightly to follow the rules. . . . We were the exceptions to the rules.)

My first professional picture. Do I look casual enough
for you? Would you buy toothpaste from this girl?

The First Time I Went Belly-Up

Palm Springs during Easter weekend was a kids' paradise.
Straight out of *Where the Boys Are*. There were so many cars jam-
packed with teenagers on the main drag that you could hardly get
from one end of town to the other, which really wasn't a problem for
the kids, since all they wanted to do was drive slow and pick up each
other. Preparation for the weekend was a major event in itself. All
my girlfriends would go shopping for their outfits weeks in advance.
This one Easter I talked my mom into letting me go with the rest of
my friends to this very hip, very expensive store. I was so excited.
My friends loved my mom, so they thought it would be great if she
came along with us to the store. We all walked into the store talking
and laughing, and there it was, the *magic outfit!* The outfit that would
turn a humdrum weekend in Palm Springs with your parents into a
heaven-on-earth weekend with Troy Donahue in Fort Lauderdale.
And I was staring at it! My mom and I stood and ooed and aahed for
about thirty seconds, which is the minimum amount of time for
these things. It was an incredible outfit, with a crop top and
straight-leg, hip-hugger pants. My mom knew a masterpiece when
she saw one, and she immediately said I could have it. It was powder
blue, trimmed in avocado green. My mom liked mine so much she
decided to get one for herself. Hers was green, trimmed in blue. She
also bought me a pair of little blue sandals with heels to go with it. I
remember trying that outfit on and becoming happy beyond belief.
It was like the feeling I had when I got my first fringed jacket and
pair of blue suede penny-loafers. Clothes made me feel free and
unique. None of my friends were allowed to wear crop tops because
they showed your whole stomach, but my mom must have been
comfortable with it because I already had a bikini. "Oh, you look so

sweet in that," she kept saying. "Just look at your little body." She was definitely the Billie Burke of the '60s. Needless to say, I knocked them dead in Palm Springs that weekend and had a *bitchin'* time even though Troy never showed up. ⟿

The First Time
I Knew the Color Barrier
Must Be Broken

When television started to cover the civil rights sit-ins down south, I got pissed off and really frightened. They were just kids getting the shit knocked out of them by huge cops with big billy clubs. What I couldn't understand was, how did the cops get away with beating these people bloody? These mean bastards dragged these kids kicking and screaming down the street or blasted them up against a wall with firehoses. These big, beer-drinking, pot-bellied, Rod Steiger in *In the Heat of the Night* wannabes and their huge fucking *Cujo* dogs were attacking all of these poor defenseless young people. And for what? Just because they wanted what should have been theirs by right anyway?

I was blown away; I couldn't understand it. It was like the time in fourth grade when I saw pictures of the Holocaust in the *Encyclopaedia Britannica* and just went to pieces. How could these cops be doing those horrendous things to people who were just trying to sit at a lunch counter? They were grown-ups—how could they do shit like that?

I was furious, crazy, outraged, but I wasn't sure what to do. I went to my mom and said, "Jesus Christ, Mom, we've got to do something. This just isn't right."

To her credit, my mother never stood for people using racist words or telling racist jokes. But she also had no solution to what was going on. Even though she was clearly upset, she would say, "It's happening far away. And yes, that George Wallace is an idiot, but there isn't anything we can do here in L.A. I was angry and impatient with her. I wanted her to be as outraged as I was. I wanted her to *fix* it.

I was rebelling against society by then anyway, and all of this just proved my point: "Grown-ups are full of shit." ～◠

My First Allergic Reaction to Republicans

I didn't like Ike. He played too much golf for my taste and way to much for a president. I also *hated* Mamie's bangs, which for some reason she plastered flat to her forehead. *Why did she do that,* I wondered. I'd never seen anybody else with that look.

As the 1960 elections rolled around, I realized I was in love with John Kennedy. He was young and handsome, and I thought he would change things; bring new energy and fresh ideas to our country. I was also incredibly impressed with Jackie. She was beautiful and dignified and dressed so modern, unlike Mamie, who looked like a Republican version of Moe *(the follicly challenged member of The Three Stooges).*

When my mom (who I will never forgive no matter how many times she swears she did it because of the *"onset of menopause"*) went out for Nixon, I was mortified. No; mortified would have been about a hundred steps up from the utter humiliation I was feeling. She was stuffing envelopes and having "strategy" meetings with the other women in the neighborhood. Soon our house was filled with Nixon buttons, placards and banners. My mom even wore a straw hat that said NIXON above the brim. What was she? . . . out of her fucking mind? I could not believe that a member of my family was doing this.

I thought Nixon was creepy and smarmy *(Cher, the clairvoyant).* And what about Pat Nixon? She was pinchy-faced and always wore those round virgin pins. (Why? She was *married*—or was this just some kind of accessory cry for help?)

I argued with my mom about it all the time. I kept saying, "How can you come out for this man? And by the way . . . get rid of that stupid straw hat."

Old, stupid, nerdy, bullshit-dressing, pinchy-faced, golfing, bad-hair-day people. I couldn't bear Republicans, even then.

The First Time a Shooting Star Ran into Me

I got my driver's license as soon as I turned sixteen, a very big deal for me; now I could borrow Gilbert's Skylark and get out of Encino. One night I drove to Hollywood and I was passing Schwab's Drugstore when a guy in a white Lincoln convertible cut me off—he actually ran me off the road into Schwab's parking lot. My heart was pounding and I was shaking because I knew if I got one dent in Gilbert's car, I'd never get to drive it again.

After the Lincoln followed me into the lot and the driver got out, I lit into him: "Are you nuts? You almost hit my car. Are you crazy?"

Then I looked at his face, and I thought: My god, it's Warren Beatty. He had glasses on, but I still knew it was him.

"I'm really sorry, I didn't think I was that close," he said.

And I said, "Do you have a cigarette?"

"No, but I can run across to the gas station and get you some."

Warren was already a big movie star. But he wasn't like any of those other pretty-boy types; he was really talented.

When he came back with the cigarettes, he asked me my name. "My name's Warren," he said. "Do you want to get something to eat?"

At first I said no, because I had a midnight curfew, and then I remembered how crazy my mother was about him, and also my best friend, Penny, so if I didn't go and get something to eat with him, would I in effect be cheating these women? While I was mulling it over, he said, "Do you want to go to my house and get something to eat there?"

I was free-spirited, and this was my first encounter with someone famous, so I said okay and went. Warren was unbelievably handsome and funny. He had a charm coming out of every pore, which is always a deadly combination.

I followed him in my car and we drove up to Truesdale, to a white modern house with sliding glass doors in back that looked out onto the swimming pool. I knew Warren was with Natalie Wood at the time, and I wondered if she stayed there, too.

Warren served me some cheese and crackers, and a Coke. I prepared myself for what I knew was coming. When he started to kiss me, I thought, "Well, this is interesting." I was fascinated by him. (But I knew a girl once whose claim to fame was that she once fucked Ringo, and even though I hate to admit it, I was doing the same thing.)

I got home around two o'clock in the morning. Gilbert was waiting up for me—and boy, was he pissed off. He ordered me to go straight to bed. The next morning, I went to my mom and told her that I'd met Warren Beatty; I just said that we'd gone to get something to eat, but I left out the rest.

The next day Warren called my mom to try to get me out of the trouble I was in for coming home so late. I don't know exactly what he said, but I remember that she was very impressed. He definitely charmed her.

Gilbert was less in awe. "I don't care who this guy is," he said. "What is he doing, going around with a sixteen-year-old girl?"

"He didn't know," I said.

"You lied?"

"Yes," I said. "What was I going to tell him? That I'd just turned sixteen and had only gotten my license the week before?"

Meanwhile, my mom was grilling me for details: "What was he like? What did he say? Was he funny? Was he as handsome in person?"

I'd told Penny the whole truth, but she didn't believe me until my mom told her about the phone call. Then they both started looking at me like I was a completely new person. I wasn't a new person, obviously. I'd just gotten some fame on me.

During one of their conversations my mother told Warren my real age, and the next time I saw him, he asked me, "Is it true?" "Yes, it's true," I said, "but I didn't want to tell you, and I'm really sorry you know now."

"It doesn't make any difference," he said. It actually seemed to make him like me more. (*Duh*—of course.)

Warren was different than any person I'd ever met. He wasn't conventional or pedestrian. He had this huge, charismatic personality, and it was always out there, with no apologies.

He thought I was a weird kid. I was. We'd take showers and talk, and he'd tell me great stories about all the things he was doing, and he'd laugh at my stupid stories. I think he got a big kick out of the fact that I wasn't interested in falling in love with him, or asking him how he felt about me, or when he was going to call me, etc., etc.

To me, he was a famous, charming movie star that I'd hang out and have sex with. This wasn't really like me, and I never did it again. Not because of any moral reasons, but because sex without love just didn't work for me—I needed to feel something in my heart.

I hadn't seen or talked to Warren for about eight months. (Son and I were crazy about each other by this time.) When Warren called out of the blue and asked me to meet him for dinner, I told him I couldn't meet him because I was in love. When I told Warren about Son, he said, "*Great.* How about lunch?"

My First Acting Class

By the time I reached eleventh grade, all my girl-friends had graduated. I just couldn't deal with school anymore, and so three weeks into the term I quit.

I wasn't sure what to do with myself, but my parents said I couldn't just sit around the house and do nothing.

I had always wanted to go to acting class. I wasn't sure where it would lead, but I wanted to try it. My parents took me for an interview with Jeff Corey, a serious actor who in the '50s had been blacklisted during the House Un-American Activities Committee/McCarthy hearings. For a while he couldn't even teach because he wasn't allowed to hold any meetings. He was a brilliant teacher, and his students included actors like Anthony Quinn and Jane Fonda.

Jeff was seriously tall, with a thin face and a beaklike nose, combined with gigantic, bushy eyebrows. He also had lots of unruly hair that stood up. He could be a little intimidating. The first time I met him (at his small Hollywood studio), he looked at me and said, "I don't take children. How can you act? You don't have any life experience to draw on."

I said, "Are you kidding me?" and proceeded to unload on him. I informed him that age and experience had nothing to do with one another. Then he handed me a copy of Steinbeck's *Of Mice and Men,* and he said, "Read this book, then come back and tell me what it means."

I read the book as soon as I came home. I thought the girl with the unbuttoned blouse was a bitch, and it broke my heart when Lennie said, "Tell me about the rabbits, George." I thought it was a wonderful, gut-wrenching story, but I was freaked out because I had no idea what it *meant!* I kept thinking, *Oh shit, Jeff is right! How can I act? I don't know what "Tell me about the rabbits, George" really means.*

But when I came in the next week for my first class, he never even asked me about the book. I wound up taking two classes a week. I was the youngest student Jeff had; everybody else was in their twenties or thirties, which I thought was ancient.

Jeff's teaching was all about finding a personal truth in everything you did. He also stressed spontaneity and *really listening* to the other actor. He didn't want you deciding what you were going to do before the scene started. You had to listen to act. (This remains my best acting skill.)

In the beginning, the other students didn't take me seriously; they saw me as a kid whose father brought her to class. But once I started to work, all that changed. I lived for class. Actually, I lived from class to class. It was definitely a turning point in my life. At last I was good at something; I could make people feel.

My favorite thing to do in class was the improvisations. Jeff would give you an exercise on the spot: "Tell a happy story. Tell about something that happened to you last week. Act out a sad pantomime." He had a million exercises, and for me it was always like playing a game (it still is). It wasn't work—it was fun. Unless Jeff got angry, and then it was horrible.

With Jeff and me, it was love and hate. One night he'd tell me I was great, and the next time he'd go off yelling, "Goddamn it, Cher, stop fucking around!" But I noticed that he had me do something in every class. One Saturday, after I'd done something onstage, he gave me a big bear hug and kissed me on the forehead. I was walking two feet off the floor. Because I wanted to be really good, I wanted Jeff to think I was special.

The First Time I Laid My Eyes on Sonny Bono

I was sixteen years old and dating a great guy named Red Baldwin. Red was a record-promotion man, an old "jazz cat" who took records around to different radio stations, to try to get them played. He had light reddish hair and a crinkly red beard, and when he laughed he'd squint till you couldn't see his eyes.

One day Red told me, "I have a great friend who just split up with his wife. He's a weird guy, but he's a lot of fun, and everyone loves him. Maybe you could introduce him to your roommate, and we could double-date." So we all decided to meet. One afternoon at Aldo's Coffee Shop, a hangout for radio people and disc jockeys who worked next door at KFWB, Red and I sat down at a table with Melissa, my roommate. Then someone came in, and everybody turned around. The room started buzzing—"Sonny's here!" "Hey, Son!"—and that's when I got my first look at Salvatore Phillip Bono. I will never forget it, because everyone else in the room disappeared, just washed away into some fuzzy soft focus, like when Maria saw Tony at the dance in *West Side Story.*

I stared at Red's friend and thought, *That's the strangest man I've ever seen in my life,* because Sonny was *Sonny* long before we were Sonny and Cher. He had this weird hairstyle, somewhere between Caesar and Napoleon. He was wearing a mustard-colored shirt with white collar and cuffs, a mustard tie, tight black mohair pants, and black Cuban-heeled boots. I was fascinated by anything different, and I was fascinated by Son from the moment he walked through the door. And I actually thought to myself, *Something is different now. You're never going to be the same.* As he walked through the coffee shop, smiling, Son immediately became the center of attention. I could see that everyone liked him. Red waved him over to our table and patted him on the back, and he sat down with us. Sonny smiled at me, but he pulled his chair up close to Melissa.

All the other guys crowded in around Son to play liar's poker, that game you play with dollar bills, and it was obvious that Son was better at it than anyone else. I just stared at Son; he was mesmerizing. His hands were beautiful. His fingers were long and tapered, and I was transfixed by his flat-linked gold bracelet, with a watch where the ID band would normally be.

That night, the four of us double-dated at what is now Club Lingerie, at Sunset and Wilcox. Sonny was gaga over Melissa—she was a knockout, with legs that began under her armpits. He thought I was some funny kid. But Red and Melissa didn't dance, so Sonny and I danced and laughed all night long.

The next morning, I woke up and I knew it was over with Red. I broke up with him that day, and it wasn't because I thought I would end up with Sonny. It was that if I could be attracted to someone else, I knew it was time to move on; I was a serial monogamist.

The First Time We Were Cher and Sonny

Once Sonny moved into the building next door to mine, he started coming over all the time. Our apartment house was a total dormitory, filled with beautiful women, and Sonny made friends with all of them. One girl was a topless dancer, another was an actress, and there were a couple of Vegas showgirls. They all had incredible bodies and long legs and big tits. Everyone had them, except me; I had a shape like Olive Oyl.

One day Sonny was rounding up some girls to go to the beach. He asked me after he'd asked everyone else, and I remember him running down our hallway as I stepped out in my bathing suit. He took one look at my skinny body, and his whole face fell. "God, you *are* skinny," he said. "But you can come anyway."

With all those girly girls around, Sonny didn't think of me as a real "girl" at all. I was this quirky, Holly Golightly free spirit with what Sonny called "a smart mouth," which was something he didn't much like. I, on the other hand, thought the sun rose and set on his ass. It wasn't quite a crush yet for me, it was more like hero worship. I just loved hanging around with him. Sometimes I would go into his closet and pull out things for him to wear. I loved watching him get dressed up in his collarless jackets, or his black sweaters with pushy-up sleeves that he'd wear with no shirt underneath. "You should wear this today," I'd say. Or, "That would be so cool." I thought he was the be-all and end-all and talked to him endlessly about everything.

When I got kicked out of my apartment, I went to Sonny, crying. I told him, "I have no place to go, I don't have a job, and I don't know how to do anything." By then I was sobbing.

Son just looked at me for a moment, then he said: "You can stay with me." I was a little nervous at first. But then he said: "I need someone to cook and clean, and also, I don't find you terribly attractive."

Well, I thought. *But you didn't have to go* that *far.*

The First Time My Mother Threatened to Throw Son in Jail

I moved into Sonny's place with my complete wardrobe: one dress, two tops, two pairs of pants, an orange corduroy coat, a pair of boots, a pair of high heels, tennis shoes, and a pair of secondhand sandals. (It seemed like everything I owned was orange, a color I won't wear to this day.) I still had only two bras; I owned so little underwear that I wound up having to borrow Son's Fruit of the Looms more than once.

I'd been sick with hepatitis and was still weak, so Son started out by taking care of me—that's the relationship we had. There were twin beds in his bedroom, and nothing happened between us. Once when I had a terrible nightmare, I went over and nudged him awake. "Sonny, I can't go back to sleep," I said. "I'm afraid."

And he said, "All right, get in bed with me—but don't bother me."

Sonny had girls coming in and out at all hours of the day and night, or calling him on the phone, and when they asked who I was, he'd always say, "Oh, that's just Cher." Late one night, one of his girlfriends came over drunk. She bounded into the bedroom and started jumping on Son's bed—and then she looked over and saw me in the other bed and screamed, "Who is that?"

"It's just Cher," Son said. "Now get outta here. You're drunk."

I loved living with Son, but I was still only sixteen and had to tell my parents a big lie.

I told my mom that I was living with a stewardess. So whenever my mother came over to visit me, I bundled Sonny's clothes up and walked down a side path to Melissa's building. She always left her living room window open for me, so I could throw his stuff into her living room in an emergency. I'd make three or four trips, running like a crazy woman, until everything was gone. Then I'd tell my mom that my roommate was away on some flight to New York or Hawaii. Then, after she left, I'd bring Son's clothes back.

The problem was, I started losing things. One day Son came into the apartment with a shirt, some underwear and one sock in his hand, and he said, "Cher, you have got to stop doing this." He'd found his clothes on some bushes in front of our apartment building. He'd also found out that I wasn't eighteen years old, which had been my story all along.

I said, "Well . . . that's true. But I'm seventeen, and in two months I'm gonna be eighteen."

I was just coming out of the shower one morning when my mom showed up unexpectedly. When I heard her at the door, I panicked. I grabbed Son's undershorts out of his sock drawer, and I ran to the kitchen and threw them in the tea cupboard—as if the underwear was the only item that could blow a hole in my story. I let my mom in, then I went back to get dressed. I heard her call out, "I think I'll make myself some tea." I heard her opening the kitchen cabinets!

I ran back out to the kitchen and threw myself against the tea cupboard, and I said, "Mom, when I come to your house, I don't go into *your* cabinets. You sit down and let me make the Goddamn tea."

Of course my mother knew then that something was wrong. The jig was up. I had to tell my mother that I was living with Son. And I had to tell Son that I'd only be seventeen that May, not eighteen.

My mother was furious. She talked about putting Sonny in jail. I said that Son hadn't known my age, which was the truth, but my mom said, "Yeah, well he knows it now." She told me I would have to move into the Hollywood Girls' Club, where men were not allowed past the lobby.

Up to this point, the warmest thing that Son had ever said to me was that I was a pain in his ass. But when Son started to help me pack my meager belongings, he just looked at me, and we both started to cry.

The First Time Son Came Home to Meet the Family

My mother's therapist advised her to let my relationship with Sonny run its course. "If you try to tear your daughter away from him, you'll only be making the bond between the two of them stronger," the therapist said. "If you let it go, it won't last two months." (What a flaming asshole *he* was. You'd be better off going to Jeffrey Dahmer for therapy than this schmuck.)

But when I told my mom that I loved Son and wanted to be with him, she made me leave the Hollywood Girls' Club and come back home to Encino, where he wouldn't have such easy access. When I got home, of course, I was hysterical. I wouldn't eat. I wouldn't talk to anybody except my sister. I couldn't sleep. I was just a mess. So my parents broke down and decided to invite Son to visit me in Encino, in a controlled environment.

He came in his buckskin pants and squaw boots. My mother was pleasant to him. My stepfather was pleasant to him. My sister adored him.

But my grandmother took one look at him and his Prince Valiant hairdo and said to my mom, "What is *that* in the living room?"

The First Time I Hit the Wall of Sound
—or—
Travels with my Rant

In early 1963, Sonny landed a job as Phil Spector's West Coast promotion man. Because of his unique "Wall of Sound," Phillip was huge at the time. He was the "Wonder Boy" and Son wanted to learn everything he could about producing from him. Gold Star Studios on Santa Monica Boulevard was the only place in town where Phillip would record. Son did everything for Phillip, from parking cars and fetching coffee to playing percussion and singing backup. And Phil was tough on him.

I'd never been in a recording studio before, and the first time Sonny took me to Gold Star, I didn't know what to think. The famous Studio A had awful lighting and a funky old couch with the stuffing coming out of it. If you went from Gold Star to any other studio, like Capitol or Columbia or RCA, you'd think you were in heaven. But Phillip loved the sound he got in Studio A, and that was that.

It was a small room, but Phillip would cram it with every studio player in the universe. He'd always have two pianos and at least four or five guitars, some electric, some acoustic. He'd bring the horns and strings in later to overdub.

I'd met Phillip the year before, when Nino Tempo (a singer and best friend of Phil's) took me up to Phillip's apartment. Phillip had been taking French lessons, and he thought he'd try his French out on me. The first thing he said to me, in French, was, "Do you want to go to bed with me?"

I answered him, in French: "Yes—for money." So we had a very weird relationship from the start.

Phillip was basically a spoiled brat.

And I thought he looked like a little drowned rat, but he was cute, too—there was something about him I liked. And there must have been something about me that he liked because he was always needling me, and he didn't even bother talking to most people. When he'd start in teasing, I'd come right back at him. Who was this skinny runt to get smart with me? I didn't work for him; I didn't give a shit what he thought about me! I wasn't about to bow and scrape to Phil Spector, the way everyone else did. But even when the four-letter words were flying, Phillip would still let me hang out in the booth with him.

The two of us kept squabbling until one day when Son finally said, "Cher, you have got to stop doing this—I work for him. Either you stop it or I won't bring you to the studio with me anymore." I knew then to shut my mouth and just watch the sessions.

I believe Phillip really was a genius, but there was a downside. He could be a real dick. He could be a lot of fun, but when he was in a bad mood, everyone in the studio walked on eggshells. People were in awe of him, and they did what he said.

Except for Darlene Love. Darlene had this big hearty laugh, and she spoke her mind. If she didn't want to do something, she'd just say, "Oh shit, *no,* Phil." Darlene didn't budge; Darlene was Darlene. She had Phillip intimidated.

I actually think Phillip was happiest when he was recording. He liked his artists a lot, though he tried not to show it. Almost all the groups that Phillip produced were based in New York. But he was cheap so he'd just fly the lead singer of the group out to record at Gold Star. Once or twice he brought all of the Ronettes in, but most of the time it was just Ronnie Bennett, Darlene, Gracia, Fanita, Sonny and me singing backup.

I always loved hanging out, waiting for Son to finish his work. So I got pretty friendly with all the guys. Leon Russell, Barney Kessel, Hal Blaine, Glen Campbell, Tommy Tedesco, Billy Pitman, Carol Kay, Lyle

Ritz—all the great studio musicians who played at Gold Star in the '60s. (Which was out of character for him; he was shy and quiet.)

I remember one time when Leon came in drunk. He was so out of his mind that it was unbelievable, and we were all laughing. Phillip was laughing, too, but he was also trying to keep the session together. Finally he said, "Leon, did you ever hear of the word 'respect'?"

Leon got up on the piano bench and said, "Hey, Phil, have you ever heard of the word, 'Fuck you'?" The whole session just died. Even Phillip fell on the ground. When I think back, those days were some of the happiest ones I can remember.

My First Job as a Baby-sitter

Son worked for Phil Spector, and after a while, I got a job with Phil, too: taking care of Ronnie Bennett, the lead singer of the Ronettes and Phillip's girlfriend. With their long hair and dark eye makeup, the Ronettes were the first really sexy girl group. They were beautiful, and they all had great bodies, great clothes, and great style.

Ronnie had one of those unmistakable voices that you'd know in a second. She was cute, fiery, and joked all the time—she also had a great laugh—and Phillip was both condescending toward her and insanely jealous of her. I couldn't understand it. Ronnie could be a little bit flirtatious, but that was just her. She was crazy about Phillip, and I never saw her do anything out of line, but he treated her like she couldn't be trusted at all. Like a piece of property.

When they were in Los Angeles, I was the person Phillip trusted to "baby-sit" Ronnie. When she wasn't needed in the studio, I'd pick her up at their hotel and take her shopping or to lunch or to a movie. We did afternoon "stuff," but there was no night "stuff." One time we got back to the studio two hours late, and Phillip was furious. So was Son, since Phillip was taking it out on him. We were never late again.

Once I asked Son, "What's going on with them? Why does he treat her this way? She has no freedom whatsoever." He said, "That's just the way it is, Cher. Just do what you're supposed to do, and stay out of it." Of course, Phillip was so weird that anything could be chalked up to, *"That's Phillip."*

My First Big Break

I sang all the time doing housework around our apartment, or walking down the street, but I never thought I would be a professional singer. I didn't know where I fit in, even when I was doing backup. The girls sang too high, and the boys sang too low, and I was just screwed somewhere in the middle.

Then one day Darlene Love's car broke down, and she was late to a session to sing the background on "Be My Baby" for the Ronettes. Everybody was standing around the microphone, waiting.

Finally Phil said, "Let's just start." And he looked at me and said, "Sonny says you can sing."

I wanted to do it but I was scared. I started to explain to him that even though I wasn't a professional, I felt I had promise. I could feel my heart pounding.

"Look, I don't care," Phillip said. "I just need some noise. Get out there."

Son said, "Don't be nervous, just do what the rest of us are doing."

I'd never been in front of a microphone before, but I went out there, quaking and shaking, and stood next to Son. I was terrible with harmonies, so I just doubled Son's part. I was terrified, right up until the end of the song.

Actually, it got worse near the end, because I knew that Phillip liked to follow a take by asking everybody to sing their parts, one at a time: "Fanita, what are you singing? Gracia, what are you singing?" I thought, *If he asks me what I'm singing, I'm gonna die on the spot, because I have no idea what I'm singing.* But he never asked me, thank God!

After it was over, I was beside myself; this was the real thing. I'd been in front of a real microphone, singing with professionals, and I wouldn't shut up all the way home; I drove Son nuts that night. "I wonder if he'll ask me to do it again. Oh, no, of course he won't but he might. What do you think he'll do, Son? When Darlene comes back, he won't ask me. I really liked it. Do you think he'll really ask me to do it again, Son, or . . . ?"

Son groaned, "God, Cher, I don't know if he's gonna ask you to do it again. Calm down before you drive yourself—and me—crazy!"

And, of course, Phillip did. He called Son and me his "funk," and for more than a year he never recorded anything without us singing backup. ～ᴏ

The first picture Son ever took of me was in Studio A at Goldstar Studio—in one of my two pairs of pants. I'm happy to be there with Son.

My First (and Last) Time as a Righteous Brother

1964 was the last time Son and I sang backup for Phillip.
It was on the Righteous Brothers record, "You've Lost That Lovin' Feelin'." They were two sweet and completely unspoiled boys from Orange County. Bill was shy, and Bobby was effervescent, and they were both ecstatic to be working with Phillip.

That song was the "Wall of Sound" at its best. It was the "Wall of Sound" at its biggest—and possibly one of the best songs ever to come out of Studio A. Phillip brought in every player I'd ever seen for that session—there must have been twenty-five musicians jammed in there. First, Phillip laid down the pianos and drums and bass and guitars. Then the lead vocals and the strings. At the end we tripled our backup parts. I was the only girl on that session. We worked on it for hours and hours, and a lot of people came into the booth just to listen.

We were there for so long, but people wouldn't leave. You could feel the energy in the studio, it was just in the air. People were walking around and saying, "This is the most unbelievable record I've ever heard."

Phillip was standing up there like a symphony conductor for more than fifteen hours without a break. Around three or four in the morning, when he decided the song was done, he played it back over and over again. We *knew*, absolutely—you couldn't not know. Everybody was blown away.

And Phillip looked up and said, "It's a fucking *giant*."

The First Time Son said, "Cher, Open Mouth, Insert Both Feet"

Son used to tell me stories about his old neighborhood, where he'd lived with Donna, his first wife. The one I liked most was the story about a woman who had sex with every guy in the neighborhood when her husband was at work. One night at Martoni's (a big music hangout that made the best manicotti in the world) we ran into Tom and Barbara, friends of Sonny's from the old days. Son invited them to sit down, and we started talking. Son was in the middle of a sentence when I remembered the story about the nymphomaniac. So I said to them, "Oh, you guys must have known the woman who made it with every guy in the neighborhood."

Tom said, "I don't think I know who you're talking about."

At that point, Sonny bumped my knee under the table, but I ignored him and kept talking. "Yes, yes, Tom, you know—the woman who screwed everybody while her husband was at work." Tom looked at me, still stumped, so I said, "Come on, Tom. Think. Son said she was the neighborhood punch board."

Tom scratched his head and said, "God, I don't remember any woman like that. Who do you think she's talking about, Barbara?"

By now, Son was kicking me, so I moved to the far end of the booth because I thought he needed more legroom. I was starting to become exasperated, but I thought I'd give it one last shot. "Look, Tom," I said. "You must remember this chick. She would do her gardening in a bikini on Son's day off and flirt with him. She was always after him. She and her husband lived next door to him and Donna."

And Tom looked at me and said, "Oh, you must be thinking about my wife, Barbara."

I got up without saying a word and went to the bathroom and never came back. About an hour later, Son knocked on the door and said, "You can come out now, Swifty. They're gone."

My First Car

Son and I moved from our apartment on Franklin Avenue to a small one-bedroom house in the Hollywood Hills, behind the Hollywood Bowl. It had a shower, and a little dirt backyard, and an ugly stain on the beige carpet in the living room. But I loved it! I had always wanted to live in an A-frame, and even though it was crummy, it was ours.

The only drawback to our A-frame was that I felt trapped up there without a car. I was stuck in the house all day long, until one day Son and my mother chipped in eight hundred dollars and got me exactly what I wanted: a red MG convertible, and it was only six years old.

There was just one problem. I'd learned to drive on an automatic and had never used a stick shift in my life. I lied to Son, of course, and told him I knew how to drive a stick. I took my sister with me for confidence (as usual), and I learned how to shift while driving downhill, which is quite a trick. Reverse was a real challenge, but once I got the hang of it, I felt so free. I'd clean up the house in the morning, and then I'd drive out to the market, or to my mom's house. I'd take Gee, or Christy (Sonny's daughter), or Ronnie along with me. I'd always take the long way everywhere I went, just so I could keep driving longer.

I was terrified to drive on the freeway at first, because everyone went so fast. Once I got over my fear, it was the only way to travel because outside of rush hours, the freeways were empty.

Even though I loved my convertible, it would constantly stall, but I learned how to jiggle two wires together to get it started again. Once I stalled out in front of a service station at Sunset Boulevard and Highland, and I got out and put up the hood, jiggled the wires and then put down the hood. I got back in and started the car—to wild screaming and applause from the guys at the service station. They didn't know there was a simple trick to it, and I got out of my car and took a bow in the middle of Sunset.

My MG wasn't a sensible car, but I loved it and took what I thought was perfect care of it. I faithfully put in water and gas, but I didn't know anything at all about oil. Needless to say, some months after I got it, the MG shuddered to a halt. I'd burned out the motor. Son was pissed. He couldn't believe I didn't know about putting oil in a car. "Goddamn it, Cher, what were you thinking?" It wasn't like we had the money to get it fixed, much less buy another car. It was a great big tragedy for me; I was grounded again.

My First Solo Recording
—or—
The Revenge of Bonnie Jo Mason

I was happy singing backup, but Sonny was dying for Phil to record me, because he was so sure I could make it as a solo artist. He kept pushing until Phillip gave in: "Oh, God, all right, I'll do it—just leave me alone."

Phillip didn't want to spend the money to record the song in Studio A because it was much more expensive, so we recorded it in Studio B, which was about as big as my fireplace.

Son gave me a great pep talk, "You can do this, you'll be great," and so on. He had all the excitement about it—I had no confidence at all. I gave an uninspired rendition of an uninspired song, "Ringo, I Love You."

Phillip released the record under the name of "Bonnie Jo Mason" because he thought that every recording artist had to have an "American" name, and Cherilyn La Piere didn't quite make it.

The single just died. My voice was so deep that a lot of people thought I was a gay guy singing a love song to Ringo, and the deejays weren't about to play a homosexual love song.

Son gave up asking Phillip to record me, and I was sure I'd blown my one big chance.

My First Real Gigs
—or—
Strike a Spare, We're Not Quite "Sonny & Cher"

Sonny got us booked on the bowling alley/roller–skating–rink circuit. Deejays like Wink Martindale hosted shows where they'd have lots of different acts come in and do two or three songs, but the deejays were the actual stars that the kids came out to see, and they were the ones who got the money.

Our first real gig was at some bad roller rink. It was then that I realized that what I thought was fear in front of a studio microphone was nothing compared to the paralysis I felt when I realized that I was about to go on stage alone and sing to strangers. Son had always thought that he would do the writing and the producing and that I would be the performer, but just as I was supposed to step through the

So happy.

curtain I stopped dead in my tracks, like a deer caught in headlights. "I can't do it," I said. "I just can't do it. I am not going out there alone. I'm just not going out there, Son. No, no, no!" So Son began physically pushing me out. But I pulled him with me because I was terrified and I wasn't going out on that Goddamn stage unless he came, too. Finally he gave up (and now that I think about it, a little too easily . . .). He said, "If you get frightened, look at me. Don't worry about the people, just look in my eyes. Look at my face." And he went out there and sang harmonies with me.

Sonny had a cute Julius Caesar haircut at the time, and he thought I looked like Cleopatra with my long, straight black hair, so we started singing as Caesar and Cleo. Onstage we wore these typical bad entertainer–type costumes. Son had a kind of lounge lizard suit, and I wore a mustard-yellow matte jersey shell top with a breakaway skirt. Just at the right moment—and to great dramatic effect—I pulled the skirt away to reveal my little hot pants underneath. It was so completely pathetic.

We were covering other people's material then, and since we had no money for charts, we'd come in early, and Son would sing down the parts to the house band, which always seemed to be five guys who played lead guitar. Some of them wouldn't know the songs, and others couldn't read music. It was a mess every time. No wonder I was scared; facing the band was enough to make you pass out. They couldn't play, and they couldn't sing backup. All they could do were bad imitations of the Temptations' dance routines.

More than being afraid to sing in front of an audience, I worried that I'd be so scared onstage that I'd feel trapped and just pass out. "What if I get so scared that I have to leave?" I said to Son. "Will I be able to leave? What will happen?" He'd always say the same thing, "Yes, Cher, you can walk off." And I'd always feel better. If you look at any of the footage of our early gigs, you'll see me looking at Son— almost never at the audience. I would sing to the people through him.

The First Time I Presided Over My Own Wedding Ceremony

— or —

I'm Here to Give the Bride Away

Son and I always felt as if we were married, even before we overcame all the obstacles to making it legal. First we had to wait until I turned eighteen, and then we had to wait for his divorce to become final. I didn't really care one way or the other if we were legally married, but Son was much more old fashioned and thought that we should just tell everybody, including our relatives, that we went to Tijuana and got married. Son wasn't the kind of guy who would open doors for you, or light your cigarette or really do anything that was considered polite in the normal way. His style of compliment was usually something like "I suppose you think you look great tonight." But Son wasn't being mean, it was just his sense of humor, and the whole time he'd be saying these ridiculous things, he'd have this little smile and his eyes would be twinkling.

One day we were in this park that we used to go to (when Son was playing hooky from work), and while some guy was playing saxophone in the background, Son said, "Don't you think it's time you asked me to marry you?" Then he showed me two silver rings that he bought at a Mexican souvenir shop on Olvera Street. His was inscribed "Cher," and mine "Sonny." Son wanted some kind of ceremony to make it official, so we went into our tiny bathroom and stood side-by-side in front of our medicine-cabinet mirror. (Don't ask me why we chose the bathroom; there was plenty of space in the living room 'cause we didn't have any furniture except his piano.) I performed the ceremony, and we exchanged rings and vows. We kissed and that was it. Then we went in to the kitchen and made spaghetti sauce, which was what we always did.

My First Meeting of
Fashion Victims Anonymous

We were driving down La Cienega, and I said, "Hey, Son, stop, go back." I'd spotted a fur vest blowing in the wind outside Andrew Mahakian's sandal shop. It was bobcat, and I *really* wanted it, but alas it was much too big for me. I made Son try it on, and it fit him like a glove. I said, "Son, you have got to have this vest. It's the coolest thing I've ever seen, it's you."

That was the beginning of our look; that vest became Son's trademark. And we found it about the same time I got my first pair of elephant bells. I'd seen this blond girl walking around with huge bell-bottoms, in a fabulous flower pattern with lots of bright colors—yellow, purple, orange, green—and the front tied up with grommets and rawhide lacing.

I couldn't get over those pants. I stopped the girl—her name was Colleen—and asked her where she had gotten them. She said, "My friend Bridget made them for me." I made a beeline to Bridget, who made me the same thing, which pissed Colleen off till we all became friends. Then Bridget made me a second pair out of chocolate-brown suede. The suede was so stiff that I could hardly move, but I didn't care. I was out of my mind with pride over those two pairs of pants. I was in heaven. Nobody was wearing bell-bottoms then.

Son and I finally made a little bit of money, and we moved up to a house above Hollywood Boulevard. We had a cathedral ceiling and a bedroom with a view, and Son let me buy new carpeting. Thank God, no more stains. After Bridget and Colleen got kicked out of their place, they moved into the apartment above our garage. From that point on, Sonny and I bought nothing off the rack. I designed all of our clothes with the girls. Son and I paid for the materials. We even bought the girls an industrial sewing machine, so they'd stop breaking their needles on our leather stuff.

Bridget and Colleen were the cutest girls, and they were also the first girls I knew who took acid. One night they came home and said, "Oh, Cher, we've been on the swings all night, and we saw people with icicles all over their faces, but you look really good. You look really warm." They were hugging and kissing me, and I thought, *Whoa, what new drug are you doing?*

After we met the girls there was no end to what I could do. I would draw and the girls would sew. It was fun designing for Son because he would wear whatever I put him in. There weren't many guys who would see a fur vest swinging in the wind and go, "Yeah, that *would* be a great addition to my wardrobe." But Sonny had always been a nonconformist, and what I was doing fit him to a T.

I made him ruffled shirts and striped pants, and put him in paisley prints and beads. One day Son and I were walking down Hollywood Boulevard, and we spotted these sealskin Eskimo boots with red-and-black-leather checked trim in a store window. It was love at first sight. When I finally got my bobcat vest, Son and I were the definitive example of the whole being bigger than the sum of the parts. We were definitely on our way.

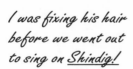

I was fixing his hair before we went out to sing on Shindig!

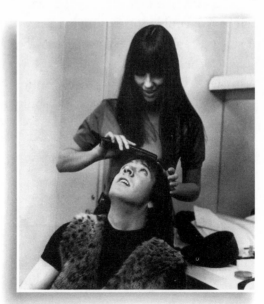

The First Time I Was "Sonny and Cher"

By the spring of 1965, we had gigs up and down the West Coast, but I made us drive to all of them in an old Cadillac because I was afraid to fly. Son would beg me to fly, but I wouldn't do it; I was just petrified.

Poor Caesar and Cleo were short-lived though. They breathed their last breath at a gig we played in Oakland. Son had finally persuaded me to fly to that gig. As the plane's door shut behind me, I almost passed out. I gripped Son's hand and cried the whole way there (what a fun trip that must have been for him).

When we got to Oakland, we found out that the airline had lost our bags. We had to perform with what happened to be on our backs. Son was wearing his bobcat, and I had on my bell-bottoms. That night at the show, when the kids saw us, they went crazy. We created a sensation.

The kids liked us the way we really looked; it was okay to be ourselves. We could stop driving ourselves crazy searching for an identity. Also, we could stop trying to come with the "right costumes." Our stage clothes were our street clothes; we were always in costume. This was the turning point for us. We went out on stage that night as "Caesar and Cleo" and came back as "Sonny and Cher."

The First Time I Was Rejected and Ejected

Sonny and I were the first hippies. Or at least we were dressing like hippies before there was a name for it. Even after we started becoming known, people's reactions were still violent. We'd be heading into a club, or finding our car in a parking lot, and these grown-ups would be shouting at us: "Dirty commies!" "Faggots!" "Lesbians!" (Now *that* is a pretty strange combo.) It was like we were murderers. I was eighteen, and I thought they were all nuts. Why couldn't they see that the way we dressed was just a way of expressing something different, new? We thought our clothes were beautiful. And we were *proud* of them.

Poor Son. He always got the worst of it; he was constantly getting into fights, but he was a scrapper. He'd had his nose broken half a dozen times as a teenager; he was tough. It got so bad that we had to hire a bodyguard named Big Jim to protect us, and then nobody fucked with us anymore, at least not after they saw Jim.

But Big Jim wasn't with us the last time we went to Martoni's, our favorite Italian restaurant. We'd been going there for years, and we were good friends with Mario and Tony, the owners. One night, as Son and I walked toward our table and past another party, an executive from a local radio station called Son a really nasty name. *Oh boy,* I thought, but Son just ignored him, and we sat down to eat. But the guy would not let it go. Over the course of the evening, he got drunker and drunker, and he kept making fun of Son's hair, clothes and masculinity.

When Son still refused to answer him, this suit man got up—and up, and up—and came over to our table. He was the tallest man I'd ever seen, at least six foot six, and he stood there towering above us. He was getting incredibly out of line with us, until Mario came over and asked him to please go back to his booth.

Then Mario and Tony turned to us and said, "Whenever you come in here, we get a big problem. We don't want you to come back, it's just not worth it."

Son and I were crushed. We left right away and never went back. We were devastated about losing Mario and Tony, who were supposed to be our friends.

After we got home that night, Son wrote "Laugh at Me." It was a hit single for him—Sonny, as a solo artist! So as it turned out, the suit man did us a favor. ~⌒ᴑ

The First Recording as Cher of Sonny and Cher

When Sonny found an old, scratched, upright piano, you would have thought it was a Steinway. "It's a great deal," he told me. "It's only got three broken keys, and they're all down in the bass end, where we don't sing. Eighty-five bucks, Cher—it's a steal!"

We put the piano in our empty living room, where Son would work late into the night. When he put down the lyric for "Baby Don't Go," the only writing material he could find in the middle of the night was a shirt cardboard from the laundry. After that he'd only write his lyrics on shirt cardboards—the white side or the brown side, it didn't make any difference.

By then we had our first managers, Charlie Greene and Brian Stone, two fast-talking wheeler-dealers, the complete New Yorker stereotype. Before we'd met them, they'd somehow moved into a movie studio lot and set up an office in a stockroom. They had telephones, business cards, stationery—they were in that room for six months before the studio found out.

Charlie and Brian wanted desperately to be record producers, even though they had no background in the business. They latched on to Son because they thought he was smart and talented. But they also believed in us, in Sonny and Cher, and they gave Son the encouragement he'd never had before.

When we needed $2,000 to record "Baby Don't Go," our managers hocked a typewriter and some adding machines; I don't even know if it was all theirs. We got some of the Gold Star guys—Leon Russell and Barney Kessel and Don Randy—to work for nothing. We used the money we'd gotten for the equipment to pay for the studio rental, the engineer, and the tape.

Sonny originally wrote "Baby Don't Go" as a solo for me, but I felt insecure about doing it alone. It wasn't so bad when I sang background for Phil Spector, because I always stood next to Son, and we laid down the backgrounds after everybody else had gone. But when I stepped into the RCA studio to sing "Baby Don't Go," I froze.

I kept saying, "I just don't want to do it by myself." Sonny knew that I usually didn't coax very well, so he told me he'd come in and join me on the choruses, which was enough to take the pressure off me. Son was like Dumbo's good luck feather for me. If he was by my side, I had the confidence to do anything.

Our First Contract as Sonny and Cher

At the beginning, Sonny didn't see us making records as Sonny and Cher; he thought he would write, produce, and sing the background parts with me. I would be the lead singer, the star. I was able to copy Sonny's phrasing, and our voices blended really well. We had a different sound from other duos, because I would sing the low melody and Sonny would take the high harmony, the opposite of what everyone else did. It happened accidentally while we were cutting "Baby Don't Go," but we kept doing it on every record after that.

After we finished "Baby Don't Go," we were so excited we ran to the record company. We wanted to play the song for Mo Ostin at Reprise (one of the coolest guys in the business). He loved it. Mo had already signed us as Caesar and Cleo, but he had no idea that Caesar and Cleo and Sonny and Cher were the same people—he didn't realize that he already owned us. When he offered us a better deal as Sonny and Cher than we had before as Caesar and Cleo, we took it.

The First Time I Heard "I Got You Babe"

We were thrilled with our first recordings as Sonny and Cher. But "Baby Don't Go" and "Just You" never made it to the national charts, though they were minor hits in California and Texas. Struggling and broke, we had to move in with my mom for a while, and then we split the rent on a funky old house with Brian and Charlie (our managers) and their girlfriends. We moved the upright into the garage, and I'd faintly hear Sonny banging out some tune into the middle of the night, until I'd fall asleep.

When he thought he had something, he'd wake me up and say, "C'mere, Cher, I wanna play you something." Then he'd give me a shirt cardboard with the lyrics written on it.

I'd look blearily at the shirt cardboard, but I could barely read it, because Son had the worst handwriting ever seen in the modern world. And I'd go, "I don't know—what is it?"

"I've got this great idea. Come to the piano." I'd try to get out of going, telling him I'd hear it tomorrow, but eventually I'd always get up. Son couldn't read or write music. He'd put the cardboard on the piano, and then he'd sing. I liked some of his songs from the start, like "Just You," which is still one of my favorites. But the first time I heard "I Got You Babe," I wasn't impressed.

"I don't think it's your best work," I said, and I went back to bed.

In fairness, Son was the worst piano player in the universe. He only knew four chords, and his left hand never moved. (When he played "Baby Don't Go," it sounded like this: "Chunk-a-chunk-a-*chunk*-a-chunk-a," and that's basically all there was to the song.) When he'd sing something new, he'd still be working out the melody, and it could sound pretty terrible.

There was a song out around that time by Jackie De Shannon, and it had a modulation, where you go up a key in the same song, which I thought was the hippest thing. I'd told Son that I wanted one. "I don't care where it is, I just want to modulate."

After Son played "I Got You Babe" for me, I went back to bed. A couple hours later he woke me up again and said, "I've got it!" He'd found a place for my modulation, at the bridge between "And if I get scared, you're always around," and "So let them say your hair's too long. . . ."

Son said, "Are you happy? I did this for you." I still didn't love the song, but I was thrilled with the modulation.

And then he said, like he always did, "Cher, sing it." He didn't trust his own voice; he needed me to sing it to tell him what the song sounded like. I was still painfully shy, and as usual, I refused, until he got cranky about it: "Cher, there's only me and you in the goddamn room. Just sing it!"

I gave in after a while, like I always did, but "I Got You Babe" still seemed like just another song to me.

My First Rolling Stones Concert

We met the Rolling Stones when they came over for their first West Coast tour. They were already popular, but it was nothing compared to how huge they would be when they left.

The Stones had to deal with a lot of square "suit people" (the artist's nemesis). So when they met Son and Jack Nitzche, they liked them immediately. Son and Jack were the only people who looked or acted anything like them: long hair, weird clothes, plus a new, low-key way of relating to one another. The Stones had finally met people they could feel comfortable with.

I'd just turned eighteen when Son took me to the Hilton to meet the boys. Son was on a phone in the lobby, trying to reach them up in their rooms. I was just waiting in a chair. Suddenly all five of them came running into the lobby like a bunch of wild Indians, but they stopped short when they saw me. I was the first girl they'd seen in the U.S. who looked like the girls back in England *(they were homesick— poor guys).*

They weren't happy with their hotel; they weren't happy with the food either: too fancy, too big. They'd order chef's salads and have no concept of what they were getting into. "We hate the Hilton," Mick said. "Why can't we come and stay at your house?" When we explained to them that we had no furniture outside of our bedroom furniture, they volunteered to get some cots and sleep in our living room.

They wound up staying at their hotel but asked if we could come with them on the West Coast leg of their tour. The next day we went with them to their gig in San Bernardino. They were very sweet, but it was hard for me to understand what they were saying because of their British accents. I'd catch about every other word. They were still kind of new at being famous and didn't have a special tour bus like the bands have now; it was just a regular bus, like the kind you rode to school on when you were little. The boys were very naïve and they stuck close together. Whenever the bus passed something they'd never seen before, they'd all move to the side of the bus it was on, look, and make hysterical comments. They were funny guys, great to hang out with, and Son and I stayed with them for a couple of days. Mick was definitely a star, you couldn't help but see that. Brian Jones was beautiful, like a little angel; those two were the most talkative and outgoing. Charlie Watts was more settled but I liked him a lot. Bill Wyman always looked older than the other boys but he had a quiet charm and was a sweetheart. All I remember about Keith at that time was that he actually looked healthy.

When we arrived at the gig, the boys went straight to the dressing room. Son and I weren't sure what we should do, but the boys said, "Don't be silly. Come in here with us!" We were all joking, just being crazy teenagers when a guy came in and said it was time for them to go on. Son and I went to the side of the stage to watch them perform. They were incredible. Their fans (mostly girls) went totally wild, and whenever they wanted to hear the girls scream, Mick or Brian or Keith would make some little hand gesture, and the crowd would go insane.

After the gig, we ran back to the bus with the boys. They were completely beat. All of a sudden, out of nowhere, all these girls were crowding around the bus. One of them was crying uncontrollably as she held a piece of paper up to the window I was sitting next to. I felt sorry for her, so I grabbed the paper, gave it to Mick to sign, and handed it back out to the girl.

Suddenly there were dozens of hands snatching at my arm, pulling me out of the bus. The boys actually had to grab me and haul me back inside. I hadn't realized how crazy it would be. When I finally got my hand back, the amethyst stone from a brand-new ring my mother had given me for my birthday was gone. Those girls had ripped the stone from its setting. I was really pissed, and of course all the boys laughed.

My First Big Trip to London

Sonny and I kept plugging away, but we couldn't quite break through. For us it was always three steps forward, two steps back. We did have the support of a few people like Jack Good, the producer of *Shindig!* Jack loved us. He was open to our strange new look and tried to get us on the show as regulars—but the network wasn't going for it. It was because of the way we looked, they said. The executives thought their viewers would take one look at us and say, *"What are they?"* We knew then that what the Rolling Stones had told us was true, that Americans just didn't get us and that if we were ever going to make it big, we were going to have to go to England. And so, in July of '65, Son and I and our managers sold our cars to raise cash for the plane tickets and, with my sister, we went to England.

I was terrified to fly, so Brian and Charlie gave me some sort of sleeping pill to get me through the trip. But then the flight got delayed, and by the time we were allowed to board I was barely conscious. I have no tolerance for medication—you can put me out with a child's dosage of anything—but the stewardess thought I was drunk and almost wouldn't let me on the plane. I was still asleep when we arrived at Heathrow the next morning. Dressed in our best outfits we went straight to the London Hilton. Son had on a Tom Jones shirt with ruffled sleeves, striped pants, his bobcat, and his striped Eskimo boots. I was wearing what I call my salute to the Union Jack, a red, white and blue top with matching bell-bottoms that had industrial zippers, and red leather spool-heeled shoes that I found at Capezio. We were looking real good, I thought. The hotel manager took one look at us and said, "We don't seem to have any record of your reservation," which we knew wasn't true, because Son saw our names on the register. He even took a picture of it for proof. "We've traveled fourteen hours," Son said, "and we're not leaving." He was pissed.

Someone must have heard about these freaks in the lobby, causing a commotion, because two photographers showed up to check it out and started shooting a million pictures of us. But the hotel didn't care and the manager actually escorted us out the front door. Later on I heard the rumor that Charlie had gotten to the hotel manager, pulled him aside, and paid him a hundred pounds to have us thrown out. I wouldn't have put it past him. Charlie would do anything for publicity. But if he did do that it was a stroke of genius.

After we got kicked out of the Hilton we started to look for another hotel. We finally found a place to stay. It wasn't as bad as the Bates Motel, but it left a lot to be desired. To start with, the water only trickled out of the shower. (Which is a bitch when you have long hair.) The bed was lumpy, the room service was frightening, and there was no TV. We were all tired, hungry, and cranky. Our fantasy of taking London by storm was not working out. Son finally blew his cool when he ordered a glass of orange juice and they brought up a thimbleful. He called back down to room service and said "Send up a goddam pitcher of orange juice and some ice cubes. I need ice cubes!" But ice cubes were like diamonds and we weren't getting any. (Actually, it would have been easy to get diamonds in our orange juice in the England of the sixties.)

When we'd gotten thrown out of the Hilton at nine that morning, we were nobodies. We had no jobs lined up, no TV dates, no nothing. No one knew who we were. But that afternoon our pictures were on the front page of the *Daily Telegraph,* and by seven that night we were famous. The British people hadn't seen anything like us before. We weren't mods (who looked like the Beatles). And we weren't rockers (who looked like an extreme version of Elvis). We were something new, and all hell broke loose. Brian and Charlie were beside themselves. Sonny and Cher were breaking out! By the second day, Son and I were swamped with interviews and photo shoots. Then the London radio stations discovered "I Got You Babe," and by the fourth day, we were asked to go on *Ready Steady Go!*—the English version of *Shindig! They* asked us to come back for the next two weeks in a row. By the sixth day, "I Got You Babe" had exploded, and they couldn't keep the records stocked in the stores.

Son and I were doing nonstop press, radio, and television, and getting no sleep. One night we came back to the hotel delirious, like kids get when they're overtired. But neither of us could sleep. I lay down on the bed and sang "I Got You Babe" to the ceiling.

Meanwhile, even though all this fame stuff was mind blowing, I was getting hungrier and hungrier. English food sucked. Then someone said he'd take us to get a hamburger. Oh yes. Oh God, yes, yes, yes. They took us to the famous Wimpy Bar, but the burgers tasted like dog food. I've never been so disappointed in my life. The situation was getting desperate. I was shrinking to a shadow of a shadow of my former self, but I was afraid of fish and chips, because a friend of mine had told me that when you threw the fish in the oil, little worms came out. (OK, I was beyond gullible.) One day I just sat down and started crying. I said to Son, "Someone's got to *feed* me!" So Son did the only smart thing, he found us an Italian restaurant. It was the only decent meal I ate the whole time we were there. Things in England have definitely changed, but it still doesn't hurt to know a good Italian restaurant.

A week after getting to London, we went to a record store to do a personal appearance. The store had expected a couple of hundred kids to show up but thousands appeared. It came as a huge shock to Son and me, 'cause we'd been so busy doing interviews in hotel rooms and TV studios. This was our first public appearance, and it was almost our last. As soon as we'd taken a few steps from the car, the kids mobbed us. They were trying to get close to us and grab some memento, but it felt like they were trying to kill us. They tore my pants and got my green clip-on earrings. (I was lucky that day because I always wore pierced earrings.) Then we heard whistles, and a bunch of policemen waded into the crowd. They couldn't control the kids, but they managed to pull us back into this car called an Austin Princess. Our new fans were rocking our car till we pulled away, and even though I was

scared to death, deep down I was thrilled because our dream was coming true.

It wasn't just the teenagers in England; the adults seemed happy to
see us, too. They were proud of the Beatles and thrilled that England
was on top of the fashion and music worlds. They felt part of the pop
scene. Once when Son and I went into a tobacconist's shop for cigarettes, an old lady said to Son, "Oh, I just *love* you two. I saw you on
Ready Steady Go! and you were adorable. Is your cute little wife really a
red Indian? Can I have your autograph?" I don't think any grown-up
had ever said that to us before. That lady stayed in my thoughts for a
long time.

Things didn't calm down any the second week, but we got to go
shopping on Carnaby Street and to go out to clubs. One night we went
to this club called The Scotch of St. James, and everybody was there. I
said to Son, "You know, Son, if a bomb went off in this place, it would
be the end of music as we know it." We were hanging out with the
biggest stars in the music business—Paul McCartney, John Lennon,
Dave Clark, Dusty Springfield, Sandy Shaw, the Stones—and they
were treating us like equals, which felt really strange because two
weeks before, we'd been nobody. By the third week, kids who'd seen us
on TV were making their own versions of our clothes. We'd see them
on the street with bellbottoms, striped pants, ruffled shirts and their
industrial zippers, or in fur vests made from their moms' coats. As we
were about to leave to go back home, "I Got You Babe" knocked the
Beatles off the top of the British charts. Sonny and Cher had arrived.

My First Shopping Spree

Once "I Got You Babe" started selling, we knew that we could spend some money. We were on top of the world, but everything had happened so quickly that to us it seemed unreal. We'd both come from nothing, and it was hard to know what the rules about money were. So I agreed that I'd tell Sonny before I spent a hundred dollars on any one thing; that seemed like a good rule.

About a week after we got to London, I went on my first real shopping spree. It was at a brand-new store called Biba. I'd heard about it through a model that one of our managers had met, and when Sonny and I got there, they were just moving things in. Their big BIBA sign was lying on the ground—you had to step over it to enter the store—and there were clothes still on the floor, waiting to be hung. (Actually, I use the term "store" loosely; it was a tiny house next door to a dairy.)

There were so many great things there. I bought two long linen tunics, with big industrial zippers up the side, one in white and one in black. And a yellow plastic tunic with the armholes cut way in. And plastic taxicab-yellow pants. It was hard for us to tell how much money we were spending, because we never got the hang of converting dollars into pounds. I wound up with six or seven outfits. I just skipped out of the store; I was thrilled. I think they cost around three hundred dollars.

We went to Anello and David, where the Beatles got their boots, and to Granny Takes a Trip, where Sonny bought some fabulous shirts and pants. I got my first fur coat, double breasted and very mod—it was rabbit, but they called it something else. (Like I would know a good fur from a bad one.) And I could finally start buying some shoes, though I was no Imelda Marcos by any stretch of the imagination. If I had ten pairs, I thought that I'd really arrived.

After we got back home, I went shopping and came back with two electric frying pans. When Sonny asked me why, I said, "Because if we ever get poor, we'll have a new one."

He just looked at me and said, "You're insane," but I think he understood. ～◯

We were like Siamese twins, only we were joined at the heart.

My First Fifteen Minutes of Fame

We got famous in about a minute and a half. Everything was fresh and strange and exciting, and there was no way that we could be ready for it. You hope and plan and work for success, but you can't imagine what comes with it. You can't even understand it once you get there. And then you find out that this thing that you don't understand is definitely a double-edged sword.

Sonny and I were nervous about coming back to America. When we left, nobody was paying any attention to us. But when we came back and landed at Kennedy Airport, Sonny-and-Cher mania was waiting for us. There must have been close to ten thousand kids out there behind the fencing, or pressed up against the glass inside. We couldn't leave the plane through the gate; we had to get off on the tarmac. You couldn't have dreamed up a better entrance.

For the longest time, a lot of those kids thought we were English, which was great for us, because the British Invasion was peaking then, and it wasn't just the Beatles and the Stones. There was the Kinks, and Herman's Hermits, and Gerry and the Pacemakers. There was Peter and Gordon, and Chad and Jeremy. You could be the world's worst singers and still get to the top here if you were English. But if you were American, it was an uphill battle.

After we got back home, "Baby Don't Go" and "Just You" were rereleased and hit the Top Twenty on *Billboard*'s pop chart. "I Got You Babe" shot to No. 1 for three straight weeks and was on its way to selling three million copies—which would be like selling fifteen or twenty million today. Son and I went on tour, but as headliners now, playing at the biggest arenas. The kids would be screaming from the moment we went on. They'd hear just enough of a song to know what it was, and then they'd scream all the way through it.

What made me nervous was getting *off*stage, because there were so many kids pushing to get up front. It was no big deal to have a bunch of kids rush up on the stage, but then the whole audience would surge forward—and since the cops didn't like us very much to begin with, they'd let 'em. There was never enough security, even when we added our own private guys, and for the last half of every show, all I could think about was how we'd get away in one piece. By the beginning of the last song, I was shaking. And by the end of the last song, I was running like hell to our car.

Sometimes we didn't quite make it to the car, and then we'd be lucky if we got out in one piece. Once as we left a gig in Long Beach, the kids pried the right-hand door of our limo so far back that it broke, and we couldn't close it. There were kids everywhere, mobbing our car. Son and I were screaming. Big Jim threw himself in back with us and yelled at the driver to take off. We had kids hanging all over the car as we drove away.

The craziest it ever got was at the Cow Palace in San Francisco, where the kids kept running onto the stage. The promoter got afraid that the stage would collapse, and he stopped the concert several times. Son sat tight, even when it got hairy, but I'd run off at the first sign that the kids might break through. At one point I was running between the stage and the car parked offstage, which was a vulnerable, open area. A security guard mistook me for a crazed Cher lookalike— one of those girls who were ironing their hair straight and dying it black, to go with their vests and bell-bottoms.

This big Neanderthal grabbed me by the throat and put me in a hammerlock. I couldn't breathe and was starting to pass out when our managers jumped on top of him and almost killed him. Brian was probably the skinniest man I've ever seen, and Charlie was short, but they were the mice that roared!

That whole show was nuts! Son almost lost all the money that he kept inside one of his socks. He was wearing moccasins that night, and the kids actually got both moccasins and one sock but they didn't get the sock with the money in it.

After the Cow Palace fiasco, I said, "I'm not doing this anymore." I just dug my heels in. Son was very gentle about it, and he took me to Sausalito. He bought me some beautiful charcoal-gray boots and a brown suede shoulder bag that I carried forever. (I've kept that bag in a frame, along with my fur vest.) We had pizza, and we laughed and walked along a misty road. He buttered me up, and I guess it worked.

My First "Really Big Show"

We knew we'd arrived when we were asked to appear on The Ed Sullivan Show in New York. I'd seen Elvis Presley and the Beatles on *Ed Sullivan*. I remembered from the time that I was little that if you were *really* important, you went on *Ed Sullivan*.

As show time approached, I was kind of in an altered state, completely petrified, and for the first time I think Son was, too. I was wearing a kelly-green, wide-wale corduroy peacoat, with a matching poor-boy shirt and my Beatle boots from Anello and David; I wanted to look totally English.

Ed introduced us as his "dear little paisans . . . the current sensations of the recording field . . . Sonny and Chur."

Sonny and *Chur?* We sang three songs on that show—"I Got You Babe," "But You're Mine," and "Where Do You Go?"—and the whole time all I kept thinking was, *I'm on national television, and Ed Sullivan just called me Chur!*

The First Time I Rubbed Bobcat
with the Upper Class

"*Jackie Kennedy is going to be at a party in New York,*" our manager told us. "And she wants you to perform."

I was thrilled and delighted. Jackie was the queen of Camelot. And we were being asked to sing at a party in her honor! But still I was confused. I asked Son, "Just how are we supposed to perform in someone's apartment?"

"Very quietly," he replied.

I went to Henri Bendel's and bought an outfit for the party: an army-green suede-cloth suit, with a short cadet jacket and tight pants that came up above the waist. The jacket had pale gold buttons down the front on both sides—I looked like a little soldier.

The apartment was in the Waldorf-Astoria. I couldn't get over all the shiny plaques on the walls and the big services that had been set out—you know, tea and coffee sets. I kept saying, "God, they've got everything in silver here." I had no idea that what I thought was silver was actually platinum and that the host, Charles Engelhard, was the platinum king of the world.

Son and I brought along a guitar, bass, drums and an electric piano. We turned everything way down, and sang very quietly for all the posh people. The acoustics were pretty good for an apartment, and we did three or four numbers, all of our hits.

"That was so lovely," Jackie said when we were finished. She sounded like Marilyn Monroe, breathy and very sweet. She was very gracious and insisted we sit down next to her. Jackie told us she loved "I Got You Babe," and that she thought we were such an interesting couple. And she then told Sonny he looked very romantic. "Very Shakespearean," she said. Jackie Kennedy wasn't a snob; she was *kind* to us. All of the other posh people were looking at us like, *What planet did these two get kicked off of?* Son and I had been invited just as entertainment, but since Jackie was being so nice, they were too embarrassed not to be nice to us, too. When she invited us to stay for coffee and dessert, the hosts said, "Of course we want them to stay. How lovely." (Yeah. Right.)

Before dessert the ladies retired into a big bedroom to touch up their makeup. I was just sitting on the bed, watching all these foofy ladies doing their thing. Even the younger ones looked older—they were so coifed, with lots of hair spray. They couldn't get over my eye makeup, which was pretty stylized. It was totally white on my upper lid, with a big black line drawn in the crease. Underneath my bottom eyelashes was a very heavy black eyeline, kind of like Cleopatra.

There was one very grand old lady who was my favorite—she loved my makeup and was really intrigued by the way I looked. She came up to me and put her hand on the top of my head, and said, "My dear, you're *lovely*. You have a pointed head."

I felt like I'd been complimented and dissed at the same time. I wondered, *Who is this old chick?* I would have thought she was nuts, except that the other women were so deferential to her, and she and Jackie obviously knew each other extremely well. This woman commanded total respect.

And then she said, "You must take pictures. Richard would love you. You must come and take pictures for me."

"Okay," I said, "Great. Whatever." I had no idea what she was talking about. I totally blew her off. Who knew?

The next day I got a call from *Vogue*. The old chick was Diana Vreeland, and "Richard" was Richard Avedon! I did my first of many photo shoots with Richard that week. I always had a little crush on him—he was, as Diana said, *Divine*. I loved working with them more than they could ever know. ～の

My First Solo Trip to the Gold-Record Store

Sonny thought that Bob Dylan's "All I Really Wanna Do" would be a great song for me to record as a solo artist. But even when I sang on my own, it was still Sonny and Cher. We did everything together.

Recording was more difficult in those days. You couldn't comp a vocal, and there were no pitch machines. You sang the song from beginning to end, and if you screwed up, you had to start all over.

When we recorded "All I Really Wanna Do," we didn't know that the Byrds were doing it, too. They were friends of ours—we used to go see them all the time before our trip to London, when they were still the house band at It's Boss. They were a great band with tremendous style. David Crosby had his green suede cape, which I thought was totally cool, and Jim McGuinn (before he became "Roger") had those weird little spectacles. Gene Clark always had this huge smile on his face, and Chris Hillman never moved—he just stood there and played his bass. And Mike Clark, the cutest one of the group, played drums. The Byrds became famous before us with "Mr. Tambourine Man," and their version of "All I Really Wanna Do" came out just ahead of mine. It seemed at that point that they'd have the hit, not me. I remember their producer, Terry Melcher, saying to Son, "I'm gonna bury you." We even thought about not releasing our version, because we didn't want to get creamed—the more bad singles you put out, the less the deejays want to play your next song. But Sonny decided we should take the chance.

When my single came out, no one believed it was just me, because I did both the high part and the low part at the beginning of each verse. The high part wasn't that high, but the low part was really low, at the absolute bottom of my range.

In October, my single reached No. 15 on the charts. The Byrds only reached No. 40.

Not long after that, Sonny had some work to do at a recording studio in New York. I was just sitting by myself out in the hall, bored to tears, playing on some old manual typewriter. When the freight elevator came up, and its wood-slat doors opened, out stepped Bob Dylan. It was the first time we'd met. He told me he liked what I'd done with "All I Really Wanna Do," which made me feel like floating away. Then he went in to talk to Son.

I just sat there with my jaw hanging open. Bob F____g Dylan. . . .

My First Brush-off by Royalty

Old Hollywood hated us. Sonny and I were making unbelievable amounts of money, and they thought we had no talent. People like Milton Berle would put us on their variety shows because they had to have a rock 'n' roll act. But they never talked to us. They treated us like freaks, like we were from another planet. They wheeled us on and wheeled us off like an animal act.

But we didn't know what a real snake pit it was until we were invited to sing at a big charity ball at the Hollywood Palladium for Princess Margaret. She had asked for us to be there, and I designed special outfits for the occasion: Sonny and Cher at their best. We were so proud of the way we looked and thought we would finally be accepted.

The whole thing was a fiasco before we ever got onstage. The show had been really late in getting started, and we were to come on towards the end. Princess Margaret had an awful headache, so she had the sound turned down before Son and I went onstage to sing. The acoustics were terrible. We were singing off-pitch because we couldn't hear anything. The sound was so bad we even started one song in the wrong key.

It was a total nightmare. I don't know if people were actually booing, but we heard something that sounded like it. Nobody was paying any attention. It had never occurred to us that the Hollywood elite didn't want us at their big event, princess or no princess. We were dying a terrible death, and I just wanted to get the fuck out of there. I was crying my eyes out, and when you get tears on crepe, it turns into something that resembles wet crepe paper. It's not a pretty picture.

Sonny handled these things much better than I did, but even he was upset that night. Our foray into this grown-up world had ended in disaster. Actually disaster would have been a day at the beach compared to what we went through that night. Who says Hollywood doesn't eat its own. ⁓

My Very Own First Death Threat

In April 1966, Sonny and I headlined a benefit concert for the Braille Institute at the Hollywood Bowl. On the bill were Jan and Dean, the Mamas and the Papas, the Turtles, Otis Redding, and Donovan. Tickets sold out as soon as they went on sale. It would have been a perfect night, except for a letter our managers had received from a very strange woman. She was some kind of religious fanatic and she said she was planning to come to the Hollywood Bowl and kidnap me or shoot me—or something equally as charming. I had received many letters like hers from the beginning. But this time our managers got really nervous, so they hired an armored Brinks truck to bring us in and out of the Bowl. I remember sitting in the back of that truck with Sonny and my sister and thinking, *This is awful. I hate this.* The woman never showed up, and the concert went on without a hitch, except that Jan and Dean acted like brats. In this kind of show, people went on in the reverse order of their popularity. Jan and Dean were scheduled to sing in the first half, but they wanted to go on towards the end, and the promoter wouldn't let them. So they got their way by showing up in the second half and then skateboarding onto the stage during somebody else's set. It was rude, but it was also hilarious. In spite of all the minor annoyances, it was an unforgettable night.

This was one of the highlights of the '60s for Son and me—headlining in at the Hollywood Bowl!

My First Papal Audience

When Sonny and I were invited to see Pope Paul VI at his summer palace outside of Rome, I had to go out and buy a dress for the occasion. At the time I didn't own one. I just didn't think about dresses, I was so into my bell-bottoms. But for going to see the Pope, I definitely felt I must have an appropriate outfit. I found a plain black dress that had long sleeves and a white collar. It looked like a cross between a nun's habit and my old Catholic school uniform. We didn't have a private audience with him; we were crowded in with a whole bunch of people: nuns, priests, little old Italian ladies. The Pope was carried in on a big throne. He spoke to everyone in Italian, and it sounded so moving that I started to get teary. He then started speaking in English, and I didn't like what he had to say because he was telling these poor little old women with holes in their stockings that they must live for the church and give their money to the church. I thought, *Bullshit. The church should be living for them and giving its money to* them. I said to Son, "I'm outta here."

My First Movie Role
—or—
Who Do You Have to F_ _ _ to Get Off This Picture?

After the Beatles came out with A Hard Day's Night,
Son got the brilliant idea that we could make a hit movie too. He met
with Nicholas Hyams, a writer, and Billy Friedkin (who'd just made a
film that had gotten a man off death row), but none of them could
come up with a story line, no matter how hard they tried. So, they decided to make a movie about Sonny and Cher trying to make a movie;
Son would go off on all these Walter Mitty tangents, becoming Tarzan,
Sam Spade and the sheriff in *High Noon.*

Son, Nick and Billy would work on the script in our living room
every night, and they drove me crazy. One night I walked in and said,
"You know what, guys, this movie is stupid, and you're stupid. It's
dumb, embarrassing, and I'm not having anything to do with it. I
didn't want to do a movie in the first place." They looked at each other
and yelled, "Bingo! Bingo! We'll take what you just said and make that
your dialogue. You don't wanna make a movie in real life, so we'll have
you not wanna make a movie in the movie!"

It was Billy's first feature film. He was twenty-nine years old and
out of his mind with enthusiasm. He always talked with his hands up
in the air—about everything. And with him and Son together, they
were just too much for me! I couldn't beat them, so I had to join them.

We had a pretty good size budget, but still we managed to run over.
Paramount pulled the plug midway through filming, and then we were
really on our own. That's when Billy, Son and the cinematographer decided to start stealing footage on the run. No permits, no nothing! We

shot scenes on a flower farm, on Wilshire Boulevard and even at the L.A. Department of Water and Power. They had a fabulous fountain that we wanted to be in a scene, so one night we sneaked in with our few lights and cameras and grabbed the shots we needed. It got so bad that we resorted to filming the rest of the movie in our own house.

I was just playing myself in the movie and I wasn't very good. My heart wasn't in it. But Sonny was hysterical, really funny. I was the straight man while he did all the outrageous comedy. Lots of times there was no script, and we just had to ad lib.

George Sanders was hired to play a movie tycoon, a suave, one-dimensional villain. It seemed to me like it was such a comedown for George (who must have needed the money, because he was much too great an actor to be doing this silly role). He was very kind to me and, of course, too good in the part. I can't imagine what must have been going through his mind.

George was the one who explained *déjà vu* to me. I was talking with him on the set one day, when all of a sudden I looked at him and said, "It feels like I've been here before, said all of these things to you before." He looked at me, and in his posh, English way, he said, "Cher, my dear, it's simply *déjà vu*."

Good Times opened in April '67, in Austin, Texas. There was a huge publicity hullabaloo: a marching band and parade, and contests for kids to win free tickets. We came in on a chartered plane, the Sonny and Cher Express. The movie did well in Austin, but it bombed everywhere else. (Today it could easily be a cult classic, if anyone ever re-released it. It's like the movie *Airplane*, stupid and hilarious.) Son and I had started the film when we were still really popular, but we took so long to make it that, by the time it was ready to come out, Son and I were no longer popular. I was disappointed, but I hadn't expected much. Son was hit much harder; he was really down for quite a while. He had put his heart into it.

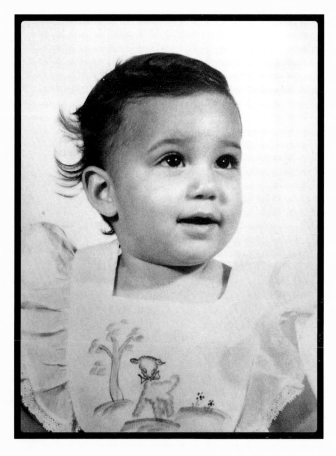

Would someone please sew some
sequins on this stupid lamb?

*I left the house right after this picture
was taken and drove over to Warren's.*

Me on my 16th birthday—
a $100 bill in my hand.

The first picture ever
taken of Sonny and me—
at my home in Encino.

This was a publicity picture
for _Good Times_. When
I look at this movie I think
Son is hilarious.

→

A very early picture
of Sonny and Cher.

I forget how young we both
were. We'd both been searching,
driven by some need to succeed.
Son knew together we would!
He was almost never wrong.

It's a good thing that we were so entertained by each other because we were constantly together.

→

Sonny and "Chur" on Ed Sullivan.

Son said, "Bobby is the answer for the country." And I still believed that the government was there "for the people."

Chas was such a happy baby. Thank God, because she was the only thing that kept us going while we were playing the Nightclub from Hell Circuit!

My angel.

Chas sitting on her dad's lap on one of our gazillion airplane trips. I can tell by his finger position that he's telling her the story of the "Good Princess Garbage and her Magic Garlic."

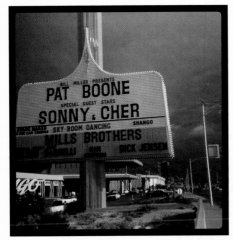

This was a big step up for us—you can imagine where we'd started from! The only good thing about this gig was Pat Boone.

Chas, the only light on our long road back.

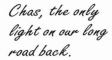

*Me on my tricycle,
being pushed by my
favorite playmate.*

*Son took this picture of my
mom, my sister and me in
our dining room on Christmas
Day. Look, I'm wearing my
cooking earrings.*

El Primo and Prima Dona on the fair circuit. Boy, was it hard for me to bend down and shake hands in this little number!

I trusted him, he was a man who was truly dedicated to helping the people. His reward for this was being ridiculed and humiliated by Congress. You really gotta respect those guys!

Method Minnie.

He might have been a Republican, and a bad actor, but he had a certain charm that you just could not escape.

Son always called Chas and me "his women." He'd walk in our front door and yell, "Where are my women? Bring me food and drink and fresh horses for my men."

← Me dressed up as my character Laverne. She was my first creation.

Son was looking for his cue cards. He never studied the script, but his fumbling around and ad libbing was what made him so funny.

One of my favorite pictures—see how cute Son is as the "Cowardly Lion."

It's not easy being queen.

This elephant's name is Margie. She was my pal; I got to ride her all over Africa U.S.A. By myself.

My First Time in the Big House with Son

We never knew how or why we got invited to a party at Tony Curtis's house. We'd never met him before, and we didn't have any mutual friends.

We weren't really familiar with the area as we made our way through Beverly Hills, into exclusive Holmby Hills. When we reached Carolwood Avenue and pulled up in the long drive, I gasped, "Oh my God, Son, look at this." It was the most gigantic, magnificent house I'd ever seen.

Tony welcomed us at the front door: "My dahlings, my dahlings, come *in,* my dahlings!" He was wearing a black velvet suit and a white silk shirt and an elegant black scarf that he tied low around his neck. He was totally grand, you know—there's no one like him. I *love* Tony Curtis.

And his house was a palace. I couldn't pretend to be unimpressed by its 28,000 square feet. It was filled with eighteenth-century antiques and Venetian mirrors, Oriental rugs and marble mantels, and ceilings painted to look like the sky. The wood paneling by itself was worth a million dollars, even then.

Son and I were in awe. We spent most of the evening walking and gawking, until Tony swept up and said, "You kids really seem to like this house."

And I said, "Oh, we've never seen anything like it."

And Tony said, "Come tomorrow, I want to show you my other house."

We met the next day on St. Cloud Drive in nearby Bel Air. Tony was just as charming in the daytime: "My dahlings, my dahlings, how *are* you, my dahlings?" The house we'd arrived at was just a smaller version of the "Big House," as Sonny and I called Tony's place on Carolwood. It was a six-bedroom, stone-and-plaster Mediterranean, with the same exquisite early-1930s workmanship and appointments, the same high ceilings and huge rooms.

"I just moved out of this house six months ago, my dahlings," Tony said, "and I'll let you have it for $250,000."

Sonny and I looked at each other; we were already sold. But Tony took us on a tour anyway, all smiles and grand arm movements. He showed us the breakfast room with its copper façade which had turned to a green patina, the screening room, the billiard room, and swimming pool with a lion's-head fountain.

When we got back in our car, I just said, "Son."

And he said, "I know. All right. We'll swing this."

After closing the deal with Tony, we rented out our place in Encino and left all of our old furniture there. We decorated our new house in a very traditional way. I guess we were trying to be appear established. We were nouveau riche, but better nouveau than never.

Our families were tongue-tied when they first came to the St. Cloud house. Son made a fabulous barbecued Sicilian breaded steak and artichokes on the arched patio—everybody ate barbecue and went around oohing and aahing.

When we were alone, we walked around in the house just looking at it. Never quite believing that we lived there. ⟿

Just a part of the "Big House."

My First Out-of-Body Experience
—or—
Sonny, Francis, and Salvador! The Three Stooges

We were in New York with Francis Ford Coppola (who was making his film *The Rain People*), Son's poker buddy, and my best friend, Joey Malouf, when Salvador Dali invited us out to dinner. We all dressed up in our best outfits, and went together to Dali's suite at the St. Regis Hotel. We were all so excited. Then we walked into what looked like a sex scene out of a bad Fellini movie. Four or five strange people were sitting around the living room, including one chick who had her breasts right out there in a see-through blouse. She might as well have been wearing Saran Wrap. I'd never seen anything like it before. Then Dali opened the bedroom door and I saw a room with rumpled sheets, and people in various stages of undress doing up their buttons.

For once Son and I weren't the strangest looking people in the room. Dali and his friends looked and acted much more bizarre than we did. They were all dressed in frilly black lace and had silver-headed walking sticks. Compared to them, we looked like we were on our way to Sunday school to teach! Also, everybody was speaking French, so that pretty much left us out.

Son and Francis sat down on a couch at the far corner of the room and picked up a coffee-table book. They were already trying to distance themselves! I sat down in a big plush armchair and tried to look as if nothing fazed me, but something was poking me. I reached behind me and found what I thought was a rubber bathtub toy: a cute little fish, with a remote control gizmo that moved its tail back and forth.

It was beautifully painted—green and blue with little orange stripes and yellow dots, like a real tropical fish.

Dali smiled at me. Then he spoke to me about the only English he would speak all night: "It's wonderful if you place it on your clitoris."

With that, Sonny and Francis lost control. They put the book up in front of their faces and hid. I could see their shoulders heaving up and down behind the coffee-table book, and they were making those squeezed little laughing noises that boys make in the eighth grade. They were just hysterical—they needed someone to slap them across the face to bring them out of it. No one else seemed to notice or care. I looked at Joey, who was still holding on, and I thought, *Okay. All right. And we're going to dinner with this man?* I immediately went on automatic pilot. I knew if I let go of myself, I would fall on the floor and pass out.

Then Dali looked at us and said, "We go to dinner now." And he and his entourage walked out the door. We followed. As we were walking down the block to dinner, Son and Francis acted like complete idiots, laughing, slapping each other and falling down. Joey and I tried for some semblance of dignity. (What am I talking about? A strange man with a mustache down to his kneecaps just told me to put a fish in my crotch and I'm trying to hold on to *my dignity!*) When we got to the restaurant, I was seated next to this woman named Ultraviolet. She was dressed in a velvet skirt and a man's shirt and tie, and she kept rubbing my leg with her walking stick. I was starting to get really pissed off. *Oh, please.* I was so *over* this dinner by then.

Dali must have thought that Son and I would be a lot wilder. Less than ten minutes after we sat down, he turned to us and said, "Excuse me, but we forgot that we have a previous engagement." And then his group got up, moved to another table, sat down, and ordered dinner.

At this point Son and Francis started banging the table. They were laughing so hard, they fell off their chairs. We all laughed 'til we cried. It was the perfect ending to a very imperfect evening.

My First Fall from Grace

By 1968, Sonny and I had fallen off the charts. It was a different time, a different sound. Jimi Hendrix was playing his guitars with his teeth. The drug culture was in full swing, and people were "tuning in, turning on, and dropping out" to acid rock—even the Beatles were doing "Lucy in the Sky with Diamonds." Son's straight-ahead, upbeat music started to sound simplistic and corny.

Kids were living together instead of getting married, and there was free love everywhere. Son and I became so old-fashioned so quickly. One day we were part of the Rose Bowl Parade, with so many fans that every last flower was picked off our float; the next day we were candidates for Geritol.

Son had strong feelings about illegal drugs and even went on public television to tell people why they shouldn't smoke marijuana. That was our death sentence, the last nail in our coffin. We were out of touch with our peers, totally disconnected.

I was antidrug, too, but I loved the new sound of Led Zeppelin, Eric Clapton, the electric-guitar-oriented bands. Left to myself, I would have changed with the times because the music really turned me on. But Son didn't like it—and that was that.

The First Time I Pissed Off
a Talk Show Host

By the early 1970s we were starting to hang out with the older set in Hollywood, people like Danny Thomas, Mitzi Gaynor, Jack Benny, George Schlatter. I especially liked seeing Lucille Ball and Rosalind Russell. Those two women in particular were idols of mine since childhood; they were the best of the best. Rosalind once told me, "You're going to be a great actress one day." I don't know what would have made her say that, but I never forgot it. Lucy knew my mom, who'd played bit parts on *I Love Lucy* for years when I was little. She was sweet and irreverent, and I was crazy about her.

On election night in 1968, Son and I were invited to Jack Benny's house. A bunch of people were sitting around the television as Nixon made his acceptance speech. Johnny Carson, who was a big Nixon fan I guess, was there, and so was one of the old Henry Ford women. But Lucy thought that Nixon's speech was boring, and she started making these great, rude jokes and noises while he was speaking. You could tell that Johnny Carson wasn't happy—actually, he was pissed off—but he wasn't going to say anything to her, right? I didn't like Nixon, either, and I couldn't stop laughing, especially because I knew I wasn't supposed to.

Son was getting nervous. "She can get away with that stuff," he told me, "but you can't."

Someone must have said something to Jack Benny that if we couldn't be respectful, we should leave the room. Jack was trying to be a good host and make everyone happy, so he said to Lucy, "You know how they are. Go sit in the den with Rosalind and take Cher with you, then you can make jokes to your hearts' content."

Lucy did what Jack asked, but she said to me under her breath, "Old windbags. Come on, Cher, we don't want to be in there with those old tight-asses, anyway." She was so right! ⟿

A Martin Luther King benefit at Madison Square Garden. I'm pregnant.

The First Angel That Called Me Mom

I had four miscarriages by 1968, and when I got pregnant again, I had to stay in the house for the first four months. I studied French and learned how to play pool.

After that stretch, I had all kinds of energy and crazy cravings. I loved Jack-in-the-Box tacos and chocolate shakes, and our chauffeur (who was having to lend us money to live on and pay our bills) would take me there in our Rolls-Royce limousine. When I wasn't busy giving in to cravings, I cleaned and rearranged furniture like a maniac. I did the baby's room in pink, blue and yellow; I was covering all my bases. I said I wanted a boy, because I thought then I'd definitely have a girl, and that's what I hoped for.

We had a couple of false labors (one of them on Son's birthday). Then one afternoon I felt some little twinges. I went to my doctor, and he said, "Okay, this is it."

I said, "No thank you, I've decided I don't *want* to do it right now." I called Son at his office to tell him I was on my way to the hospital.

He said kind of casually, "Oh, okay, I'll talk to you later."

I said, "No, Son. I'm on my way *now.*"

I got down to the hospital about six o'clock in the evening. On my way there, I noticed that the moon was huge and full—or was it the sun? I was so scared I couldn't tell. My knees were shaking, and my teeth were chattering. They put me in a wheelchair, and Son met me at the front entrance with Denis, our best friend and assistant, taking pictures of the whole thing. Son was going, "Sweetheart, later on you're really gonna like it that we have these pictures."

And I said, "Sonny, if you don't stop the picture-taking crap, I'm going to kill you."

By the time I got down to the delivery room, everything in my body was shaking. I felt better when my doctor and his nurse, Elizabeth, arrived. She'd been my closest friend during the pregnancy. Her mother had died in Sweden the night before I went into labor, and still she was there for me.

Then the anesthesiologist strolled in, looking like some fucking playboy wannabe. He was wearing a stupid little ascot and talking about how he'd been out to dinner and wished he hadn't had to come back in—"but, oh well, what the hell."

As he put the I.V. into my arm, I'm looking at him and thinking, "I don't want this asshole giving me any drugs." As it turned out, he gave me too much, and I was totally screwed up; I was pretty much out of it the rest of the time. People weren't doing natural childbirth in those days, and I certainly wanted to cut down the pain, but I'd also wanted to be conscious.

Elizabeth was rubbing my hands, and I could hear her talking. But when I looked at her, she had too many eyes. Later she told me that whenever I started to yell, I'd stop myself and say, "Cher, you mustn't scream—this is a hospital zone."

Sometime after midnight, I remember someone saying, *Push, push, push, push, push. Don't push. Push.* And then I heard a baby cry. I asked the doctor about ten times, "Does she have all her fingers and toes?" That was all I could think about. But I never saw my baby that night because of that schmuck with the ascot.

The next morning, Sonny came in and said the baby was beautiful. In the afternoon, they brought the babies around to everyone in the maternity ward—to everyone but me. I buzzed for the nurse, who told me, "I can't bring your baby down. If you want any information, you'll have to call the doctor."

I started sobbing. I called Son at the office, and all I could get out was, "Son, the *baby.*" He rushed down to the hospital, and I could hear him screaming at the doctor and the whole nursing staff all the way down the hallway: "How *dare* you upset my wife? Are you guys crazy? Who in the fuck do you think you are?"

The baby was fine. They hadn't been able to get her temperature high enough, so they had to keep her in the incubator for a while—which the nurse could easily have told me.

I finally saw my daughter late that night. She was so cute, with great big eyes and so much black hair she looked like an Eskimo, and she was so tiny. And I thought, *What am I going to do? I don't know how to take care of her—I don't know anything.* I was so nervous that I took a sleeping pill, which didn't do anything at all, and I lay in bed sweating all night long.

We named her Chastity, after the movie I'd made with Son—it might have been a huge flop, but I'd always loved the name. For her middle name, I wanted to do something special for Son, so I named her Chastity *Sun.*

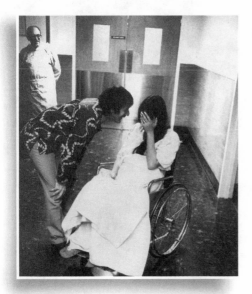

Oh, Son—how could you! Please . . .

I was happy but I was also scared stiff. I didn't know how to take care of a baby. Thank God Son was calm.

I love this picture so. It's us—so us. Sonny and Cher.

My First Nightclub Act
—or—
Son, How Much Do We Owe the IRS?

When Chas was six weeks old, Son gave me the bad news: "We're broke! We owe the IRS $270,000.00.

"Just give me two years," he told me, "and I promise you, I'll get us back up on top again." He had great faith that he could make things happen—this faith was called *Sonny and Cher.*

I was a new mother and was afraid to go back to work, but I didn't have a choice. "Okay," I said. "I'll give you two years, and that's it."

But what would we do? Concerts were out of the question, since nobody was buying our records anymore. Our only alternative, Son said, was the nightclub circuit. I looked at him and said, "What night- club circuit do you have in mind, buddy boy?" He might as well have told me that we were going to have to take a gig on Mars. We would have to perform in front of all the adults who never liked us to begin with, and there was certainly no reason for them to like us any better now. It was one of the low points of my life.

Son and I started at the bottom—the Elmwood Casino in Windsor, Ontario. We were booked for a month and stayed the whole time at a motel across the street. It was like a bad Holiday Inn, a *really* bad one, with broken plumbing and chipped paint and mildewed wallpaper. We cooked on a hot plate in our room, and a train whistle woke us up every ten minutes during the night.

When we came out on stage to sing, we were in total culture shock. Just two years earlier, we were selling out 30,000-seat arenas and play- ing to screaming fans who adored us. Now Son had to put on a tux, I had to wear evening dresses, and we had to sing middle-aged covers of middle-of-the-road music that I can't even remember now (thank you, Jesus)—I've blocked a lot of it out of my mind. We'd go on stage through the casino kitchen, watching out for the grease spots or a waiter with three bowls of soup. On a really good night, there would be a couple hundred people out there. On a slow night, we might sing to three tables.

We'd get polite applause, but I knew that nobody really liked what we were doing. I was depressed almost all the time. I didn't have much armor against the rejection we dealt with every night, and the work itself was total drudgery for me. That is when it wasn't busy being humiliating. You see Son liked to experiment with our act. The only problem with that was he liked *me* to do the experimenting. He saw me as an extension of himself—there was no line between us. We were Siamese twins; he was the twin with the brain. I was the one with the voice.

We were in our motel room one day when Sonny said, "Hey, Cher, come here." I was always in terrible trouble when he started his sentence like that. "You know that song from *Madame Butterfly?*" (I'd been dumb enough to tell him about "One Fine Day," a Puccini aria that I'd memorized as a little girl.) "I want you to sing it tonight." Excuse me, Son?

From then on, I had to do "One Fine Day" at every show, and the audience was looking at me like I was a fucking nut case. They had no idea I was singing opera. I really wanted to kill Son for that one.

The night we finally stopped doing it, a woman walked up to me and said, "I came here just because I heard you were singing *Madame Butterfly,* and you didn't sing it!" Sometimes you just can't win.

∽

The First Time Son Misplaced Our Baby

While Son and I were playing clubs, it was a perfect time to raise the baby. I could play with Chas all day and put her to bed just before our first show. Then Heidi, Chas's nurse and the sweetest woman in the world, would take over. Chas was the most adorable, good-natured baby I've ever been around, and we doted on her completely. She was so fresh and sweet, and she distracted us from the fact that we were just in a world of shit, playing all these horrible gigs.

From early on, she'd go along with her father's strange sense of humor, no matter what he did. Son used to make up his own ridiculous nursery stories for her, about Og Oggleby and the Good Princess Garbage. He had a great sense of the absurd; he even got me hooked on his stories. I'd start listening and get totally sucked in. Everything had an Italian twist to it: "And then the good princess took the magic garlic. . . ." I'd be pissing myself laughing, and Chas was mesmerized.

One time, Son told me that he couldn't find the baby.

"What do you mean?" I said.

And he said, "I don't know, she just disappeared. Let's look for her."

At that point, I knew he'd done something weird with her. I finally found Chas in Son's closet. He'd blackened her face with cork and hung her on a hook with his stretch terry-cloth pajama bottoms. And Chas was just hanging there, not making a sound, because she knew it was her dad's idea of a joke. It was her idea of a joke, too.

The First Return of "Smart Mouth"

Second shows were the worst. When you're playing a club, the first show draws people who are out for dinner and an evening's entertainment, but to pull an audience into a second show, you've got to have a real following. When Son and I started out, our second shows would consist of two people who were so drunk they'd passed out at their table and some guy who thought he was going to see a strip show.

I think it all began at one of those second shows where we were playing to about eight people, and one of them was a heckler. We got tons of abuse all the time from people who considered us freaks and were glad that we'd had our comeuppance. One night I just got fed up and fired back at this bum. Son went, "Cher, come on," so I tried to restrain myself.

The next night, some other guy said something I didn't like, and I put him in his place, but good. The band cracked up, and dealing with hecklers became my forte. I could observe the situation, make my analysis, and shoot from the hip, all in a split second. I never got too angry, because Son said that would get the audience uncomfortable. He said, "You want to make the hecklers seem like idiots, so when the rest of the people start laughing at them, they stop doing it."

But we couldn't count on the drunks and the assholes to show up every night (well OK, maybe not the drunks). So instead of just singing our songs, and Son talking about how glad we were to be there (which I thought was such bullshit), we began joking around with each other. We did it out of desperation and boredom, also for the band, who could get pretty restless by one in the morning. Nobody else in the house was paying any attention to us anyway. I got to do most of the zinging—about Sonny's mother or his height or his lousy singing. Now and then he'd zing back about my skinny figure or big nose.

*The Dynamic
Duo. Trying to
get back on top.*

(I never understood that, because Son had a much bigger nose than I did.)

This kind of banter was perfect for me; I did it all the time before Son and I started living together because Son hated what he said was my "smart mouth." He thought it was disrespectful, so I'd kept it dormant for six years.

But now my sarcasm was working for us. We'd play with the banter whenever we had a light crowd, making it up as we went along, and the band would get hysterical. As we trudged our way through the circuit—a month in New Orleans, a month in Dallas—word-of-mouth began to spread. Our second shows started filling up, and no one was bored anymore. Also, people were starting to like our singing. Our show was working all the way around.

Son and I were a perfect team. I was too shy to talk directly to the people, but Son was a natural. He became the straight man, and he'd talk and talk and talk and talk—and then I would say one line and cut him off at the knees. We were like Gracie Allen and George Burns that way. Son was the charming buffoon; I was the glamorous bitch.

My First TV Show with Son

By 1971, Sonny and I had done several guest shots on TV. But I didn't see television as some big career move for us.

That spring we were playing the Americana hotel in New York. Our act really worked by then, and we just happened to be brilliant that night. Thank God I didn't know that Fred Silverman from CBS was in the audience; Son knew better than to tell me. I'm not sure I could have handled the pressure.

Freddie loved our act and got us a shot guest-hosting for Merv Griffin, who wanted the night off to go to the Oscars. A few days after that, Son came to me and said, "We're gonna do a summer replacement show—*The Sonny and Cher Comedy Hour.*"

I was beyond excited; now we could come off the road (or the Night Club Circuit from Hell, as I called it). I was also beyond nervous: "Son, we don't know how to do a TV show."

"We'll learn," he said.

That summer CBS was airing *The Six Wives of Henry VIII,* a BBC miniseries. Since Henry had six wives, the series had six segments. Which meant the network needed six one-hour variety shows as lead-ins.

It's a good thing Henry couldn't get it together with the women in his life, or we might never have had those six summer shows—and our big break.

Our first show was on August 1, 1971, with Jimmy Durante as our guest—it was a "nose" show. We were pretty ragged at the start, and the network wasn't quite sure they wanted to go forward with us. But Freddie put all his weight behind us. We were his discovery, almost like his kids in a strange way. He was a smart guy, and he was ready to do something that hadn't been done before.

And we were that something.

Son had faith in Sonny and Cher, and I had faith in him.

The First Season of
The Sonny and Cher Show

The Sonny and Cher Comedy Hour came back as a regular show just after Christmas of 1971. We were pulling in millions of viewers per week—our demographics were huge. Whole families watched us, from little teeny kids to old grandmothers. We loved doing the show so much, we would have paid CBS to do it

Son almost never bothered to learn his lines, and because he was so funny *not* knowing them (like Goldie Hawn on *Laugh-In*), it worked better that way. Son and I knew each other so well that many times we could ad lib lines that were funnier than the script. I would just let Son flounder, then hit him with a one-liner. The more fun we had, the more fun the audience had. The show never felt like work to me. It was always like a game I played with Son.

We had Chastity on the show a bunch of times. Son thought she should have been in nursery school playing with kids. But I said, "She doesn't like kids—she likes adults." And the guys in the show loved her. Everybody loved her. She was practically raised in Studio 31.

Also, Son and I were lucky to have guest stars who liked to get into tights and put on crazy, corny skits with us. I got to meet some of my favorite people that way, like George Burns and Douglas Fairbanks, Jr. (who was still incredibly dashing). Once I even got into the ring to trade insults with Muhammad Ali. Even though he was huge, he had such a sweetness about him.

Once while Ronald Reagan was still governor of California, we presented him with the coveted "Bono" award—a mock Oscar that was mostly nose and mustache. I'd never really thought much about Reagan before. He was a Republican and not a great actor, and those were two strikes against him in my mind (and in Son's mind, too, at that time). But I have to say he was fun to work with, a real charmer.

A family that plays together . . .

My First Mackie Gowns

I met Bob Mackie back in 1968, when Son and I guested on *The Carol Burnett Show.* I walked into the costume house where we were supposed to meet for a fitting, and this amazing young man came out of a doorway. He was tall, golden-skinned, and had blond hair in a sort of Grecian style. He was much younger than I was prepared for. And I thought he was a brilliant costume designer. Also amazingly handsome. I had always been a big fan of Carol Burnett and had never missed a show. I was also crazy about the costumes she wore. *No one* could design a costume like Bob Mackie. (He is still the best as far as I'm concerned.) Bob could design a beautiful gown and then turn around and do insane character costumes, like the one he did for Carol's "Norma Desmond." Norma was a take-off of the character that Gloria Swanson played in *Sunset Boulevard,* and Bob really outdid himself with her costume. She had these sort of long beanbag breasts that hung down to her knees, and a huge belly that also hung down to her knees. It is still one of the best costumes I have ever seen! I decided then and there at that first meeting with Bob that if I ever did a TV show, he would be the one to design my clothes. He was my dream designer. He still is.

When we had our first summer replacement shows, we didn't have any budget. Ret Turner did the costumes for Son and the rest of the show (no small feat), and we could only afford Bob for *my* costumes. There was definitely *no* money for beads. It wasn't until we came back in December that we gradually got into those beaded dresses. My first unforgettable Mackie gown was for the vamp number I did lying on the piano: a red beaded dress with matching headpiece. That gown absolutely killed me. I felt like a queen wearing it. (I don't know what kind of country would let its monarch run around in a red beaded gown with her entire stomach out, but I bet the Village People would be doing the handiwork around the castle!)

As the show became really successful, I needed at least two or three new beaded dresses per week. They cost about $5,000 apiece then (a big change from the time I came to Son's apartment with one dress). Wednesday night was always fitting night. I would come to Bob's workshop and stand for three and a half hours while Bob and Raymond and Ret and Elizabeth looked on and made suggestions. Just standing there for hours on end was hard, especially since I had already put in a full day of rehearsal at the studio. But we were doing a costume-oriented show, and it was part of my job. Millions of women watched just to see what I was wearing. As good as Bob was with Carol Burnett, people didn't notice how wild he could get until he started working with me. I was twenty-five years old, and I had a body like a coat hanger. You could put anything on me.

And I never felt self-conscious. I would never say, "I can't wear that." I'd say, "Do anything you want to do." I was also lucky that Bob was a throwback to the old Hollywood days, when every star had a look that was unique. Maybe some people thought I looked ridiculous, but that was okay by me. Look, I'd started out as a skinny little kid from the Valley. And now I'd become a one-named enigma called Cher.

When I look at these
pictures, I remember how
much fun we were having.
We were a great team in
every sense of the word.
But fame, work, marriage
and life get complicated
like a ball of knotted
gold chain.

My First Hit of Television Fame

When you do a one-hour weekly TV variety show, you don't have any life. You spend five days working on the show, and the other two days you're too dead to move. Whenever we weren't working on the show, Son had us back out on the road, doing concerts, fairs, etc. (As George Schlatter, the producer, once said, "If Sonny had to travel from the Valley into town, he'd take a gig on Mulholland Drive to break up the trip.") So between the show and the road, I really didn't come in contact with people that much.

One time when we were doing the TV show, we came in on a Monday for a readthrough, but the whole script was so terrible that it had to be rewritten. This gave me some unexpected free time and gave me a chance to go out shopping. As I walked into the makeup department at Saks, everybody just turned around and looked at me—I mean, they stopped what they were doing and stared. I looked behind me, and then I looked back at them, and I thought, *This is really strange. What are these people doing? Can't they see that I'm looking at them stare at me? Hello, I see you!*

It was the first time I'd been out where I could feel that the fame of TV was different than that of records. When you were one of the top-ten-rated shows on television, millions of people were watching you every week. I wasn't complaining. I was just a little shocked. This fame was all-encompassing. It could just swallow you up.

(But on the bright side, I did get great help in the makeup department that day.)

The First Time I Tried Marijuana

While the drug culture was busily becoming big business, Son and I were busy trying to become big show business. He was always adamant about not having anything to do with drugs, and truthfully, I wasn't that interested. After Son and I broke up, however, I was gung-ho to try marijuana. All my friends smoked it, and I wanted to be modern and smoke it too! The first time I tried it, I was at my boyfriend Bill's house. He was rolling a joint and asked me if I wanted to try it. I did want to try it but I was a little scared. But I also trusted Bill very much and thought that if I was going to smoke a joint, he was definitely the right person to do it with. Bill lit a joint and told me to take a small drag. I did, then he said, "Do it again." I did. Now he said "Just sit back and see how you feel." A minute or so went by. Nothing. Then a couple more minutes passed. I started to feel a little dizzy, but it wasn't bad. I felt okay. Bill then said that that was enough, and that two hits were probably the right amount for me, at least for now. Then Bill had to leave for an hour to do some errands and while he was gone a girl came over. She sat down and rolled a joint, then handed it to me. I didn't want to appear stupid and square, also I'd just done it and it didn't seem like any big deal, so I took it. We sat and talked and passed this joint back and forth. She was very sweet, and before I realized it, I'd smoked the whole joint with her. Then I freaked out. The room suddenly got really tall, and I felt like I was slipping away. I didn't know this girl, so I couldn't tell her how terrified I was, or that I had only had marijuana for the first time that day. I felt so bad that I decided to take a warm bath. As I lay there in the water I had a little hallucination. I could hear Sonny's voice up above me, "See, Cher, I told you this would happen if you did this! I hope you're satisfied." No, Son, I'm petrified. Does that count?

Another time my friend Paulette told me the way to have fun doing errands: get high first. We were sitting parked off Sunset Boulevard, smoking a joint, looking over our list of things to do, when I saw a police car come up and park half a block behind us. We both got so paranoid that we smoked that joint down in a second, handing it back and forth. God, we were stupid. By the time we finished it, I was out of my mind but trying super-hard not to freak out. Paul was my best friend and I always felt secure with her, but now I was really fucked up. "Relax," Paul said. "It'll wear off while we do errands."

So first we went to North Beach Leather to get two pairs of pants altered. I walked in, but I decided I didn't like the vibe, so I just handed the girl my pants and left without a word. (I never went back.) Then we went to a restaurant called The Good Earth and looked at the menu, but it had bad vibes, too, so we left. Finally we went to the shoe repair shop. This time Paulette went in by herself and left me waiting in the car. I felt as though I was waiting there forever. Where was Paulette? When was she coming back? What was she doing? Finally she showed up. "Jesus, Paul," I said. "What the hell happened to you? I've been sitting here waiting for hours. *And* that clock on the shoe repair store doesn't work. It hasn't moved at all!" Paul looked at me: "Cher . . . that's not a clock. That's the Red Goose shoe sign." ⟿

Paulette Betts

CHER'S BEST FRIEND AND
FORMER ASSISTANT

I met Cher in 1972, when *The Sonny and Cher Show* was huge and Cher was like a goddess to America. Everyone thought she had the perfect wardrobe, perfect family, and perfect life.

In the beginning, what struck me most about her was how someone who was perceived as being so sophisticated and worldly was, in real life, incredibly naïve, with the emotional vulnerability of a sixteen-year- old. I taught her a lot about what I considered to be fundamental "growing-up" stuff. I'd had a normal childhood, gone to college, etc.— all these ordinary things, but she found them exciting. She'd ask me about my life experiences all the time and I'd think, *Why do you want to know this boring stuff? You're Cher!*

It was during the first few years of our friendship that we spent the most time together—we had amazing adventures and got to know each other really well. Cher has a lot of great qualities, but one of my favorites is her ability to assess a situation (or person) clearly, before anyone else can. This talent helped me a great deal after I'd gotten divorced from Dickie Betts (of the Allman Brothers) and was venturing back out into the world of being single again.

I had started dating a man I thought my parents would *love*. Buckley was a stockbroker who wore a suit and had short hair, completely the opposite of my long-haired, tattooed, rock and roll ex-husband who'd been an alcoholic and had drug addiction problems the whole time we were married. As far as I was concerned, Buckley was exactly what I needed at that point in my life. I couldn't wait for Cher to meet him.

So we all arranged to go boating on the Gulf of Mexico, near where I was living at the time in Sarasota, Florida. I thought things went pretty well that day, but after Cher got back to L.A. we spoke on the phone. "Pauli," she said, "You're my best friend and I love you, but I'm not going to be able to speak to you for a while."

Needless to say I had *no* idea what she was talking about. I thought she was out of her mind! However, unbeknownst to me at the time, Cher had spoken to Buckley on the boat that day: "You know, right now Paulette thinks you're the best thing that ever happened to her. But I can see you for what you really are. You're the same person she just divorced—you just dress better. I know you lie to her, and I don't trust you as far as I can throw this boat. Pauli's my best friend. She's like a sister. And you're an asshole in an Ivy League suit!"

It took me about four more months to become aware of the problems that Cher had foreseen so clearly in Buckley that day. I called her up and I said, "Okay, I finally see what you were talking about, but I really think I can change him." I tried to convince her that I was right, but it didn't work—she is one of the most stubborn people I know, especially when she has an instinct about someone. But even though I just could *not* get her to agree, she still was very patient with me, and about six months after *that* (I'm a slow learner!) I broke it off with Buckley.

Cher has the clearest insights for everyone but herself, as is usually the case. When a person is that insightful about others, sometimes their own mysteries elude them.

My First Days Being My Own Boss

After Sonny and I split up, we kept doing The Sonny and Cher Comedy Hour, and we still lived in the same house together— only at opposite ends, twenty-five yards of hallway apart. I couldn't tell anyone what had happened. But I told Son that I wanted an allowance of $5,000 a month, deposited in a checking account in my name. (My first; I was twenty-seven.)

I thought the arrangement was heaven. I still loved working with Son and hanging around him, but I didn't have a bedtime anymore. I had some freedom. I actually bought a new car, a Dino Ferrari, and came to work on my own.

On the weekends I'd drive out to a beach house I'd rented, and sometimes I'd meet Bill there. One night Bill asked me if I wanted to go to a movie. I said yes. Then he asked me what I wanted to see.

I started to cry. I wasn't used to being asked.

Bill pretty much understood me, but he was a bit shocked at that one.

Me getting funky with my "bad self." Check out the nails. I'm with my friend Ara, the great makeup and hair guru of his time.

Georganne La Piere

CHER'S SISTER

In 1974, Cher, Paulette Betts (Cher's best friend) and I decided to go to Europe. Before leaving for London, we asked around for a good hotel, and everyone told us that Blake's was the new, hip place to be. We wanted to be where it was really fun, so that's where we went—and it turned out to be the tiniest hotel we'd ever seen in our lives.

We had a suite, but the rooms were built for people about the size of Munchkins. Paulette and my sister are tall, and I'm of average height, but this place was so small that when one person got up to walk around, the other two people would have to sit down. The room felt even smaller because we'd taken an *insane* amount of luggage; I think we had twenty-three Louis Vuitton suitcases, just for the three of us. (We carted those suitcases through several countries, and it wasn't until the *end* of our trip that someone finally told us that only prostitutes carried Vuitton luggage in Europe! Naturally we thought this was hysterically funny.) We were falling all over each other in our suite, getting more and more pissed off by the minute.

At one point, as Paulette was trying to cross the living room, my sister sat down on the glass coffee table to let her pass. It immediately broke in half and she fell completely through it. Cher wasn't hurt, but that was the final straw for her. It was already 10 o'clock at night but she said, "We're getting out of here!"

Paulette asked her, "Where are we going to go?"

And Cher said, "I don't care, it doesn't matter. We're just going to pack up and leave, because this is stupid."

We were thinking like Americans, of course. Like you can just pack up and move from the Hilton to the Holiday Inn at any time of day or night, and nobody would think anything of it. But in England (at that time) the "good" hotels were extremely conservative. We called around to Claridge's and a few of the other nice places, and they all wanted *references!* They didn't care that we had the money. They didn't care that it was Cher. But Cher had made up her mind, and so we packed up all our stuff and got ready to go—where, we didn't know. The "bellboy" at Blake's was about eighty years old, and the elevator was so small that he could only take down a couple of bags at a time. The poor guy had to make at least a dozen trips.

We called the Playboy Hotel next, but they also said they didn't have any rooms available. Cher said, "I bet if Hugh Hefner called you'd find us one." They didn't disagree, so Cher called Joe De Carlo, who managed Sonny and Cher in the '60s and who was one of Hefner's good friends. Coincidentally, she tracked him down at Hef's house, and when he called us back a few minutes later, he said, "Go back to the Playboy Hotel. Hef has arranged everything, they're expecting you."

We needed to get two cabs to cart all the luggage, and it was midnight by the time we got to Hef's hotel. We carted all our crap into the lobby where we were (now!) welcomed. The manager gave us a big reception and said, "Let me take you up to see your accommodations." So we rode up in the elevator and were shown into a huge suite. Unfortunately, it looked like a family of Bedouins had been camping out there for a week—the beds were torn apart, there were chicken bones all over the floor and it was absolutely filthy. There was no maid on duty until the next morning, so they couldn't even clean it for us while we waited!

By now it was at least three o'clock in the morning and we had *nowhere* else to go. We just sat on our huge mound of suitcases in the lobby, getting crankier by the minute. Cher called Joe De Carlo back to tell him what had happened, and he remembered that Hef had a friend

I was the official makeup artist on this trip and made up my sister and Pauli every night before we went out catting around. We never came home before dawn. We didn't do shit. We were just best friends in Europe, screwing around.

named Bernie Kornfeld who had a townhouse somewhere in London. Although it was the middle of the night our time, Joe D. called him up and explained our dilemma, and Bernie said, "Oh, just have the girls come over to my place, no problem."

So we took off again in two more big cabs (one for us, one for our luggage), this time in search of Bernie's townhouse. It was now close to 4 A.M., and for some reason we weren't sure of his address. We managed to find his general neighborhood and sent Paulette up to knock on (what we thought was) his front door. Five minutes of ringing the front bell later, some poor woman came down attired in curlers, bunny house slippers, and a bright pink baby doll nightgown—clearly *not* Bernie Kornfeld!

We finally did manage to find Bernie's house, and he greeted us in a short little robe that just covered his crotch—barely. It was a three-storey house, and he said that Paulette and I could sleep on the bottom level and that Cher could sleep on the top floor. We didn't know this man from Adam, and while it was lovely of him to have taken us in in the middle of the night, we were still a little wary. After all, he was one of Hugh Hefner's friends, and who knew what *that* might mean?

So we asked him if we three girls could all sleep together and he said no, the beds were too small, the rooms were too small, etc. So Paulette and I left Cher in her room at the top of the house and then went down three stories to the basement. It was clammy and damp down there, and we felt like we were sleeping in a dungeon. The decor was trying for a nautical theme, but the end result was more like sleeping in an old, musty boat. We lay there for about five minutes without speaking, and then Paulette and I turned to each other at the same exact moment and said, "Fuck *this*. We are *not* staying down here and we are *not* leaving Cher all the way up there by herself." So we went hauling ass up to the third floor, and there we found Cher *in* her bed and *Bernie* sitting *on* her bed chatting away. Later Cher told us that she was in the bathroom washing her face with a small hand towel when Bernie walked right in saying, "Hi—how are you? Got everything you need?" etc. . . . . She was clad only in her underwear at the time and didn't know whether to use her tiny towel to cover up her top or her bottom as there was no way it could hide both areas! She said she got so nervous that she just jumped into her bed—and that was where Paulette and I found her, with Bernie chatting away cheerfully in his minuscule little robe with his ass hanging out!

So that night the three of us squished into Cher's double bed—one head at the bottom, one head at the top, one head at the bottom. (Cher slept in the middle, with a pair of feet on either side of her head.)

The next morning Bernie brought up breakfast for us, and then he sat on our bed again talking. He was a strange man, but also very sweet and generous. And ultimately harmless.

That afternoon we finally got into Claridge's—it seemed that once the sun came up, we were deemed sufficiently respectable!

My First Tattoo

After Sonny and I were separated, I got my first tattoo.
I thought it would be something different, some sort of statement of freedom.

"Good" girls didn't have tattoos then—no one was doing it. I decided to get one on my butt, where no one else could see it. It would just be for me.

I went down to a tattoo parlor on Sunset and chose a butterfly with a flower. The artist was very matter-of-fact; he'd been doing this for a million years. He told me that it hurt less on the fleshy parts of the body, and I said okay, and so he started.

When you get a tattoo, they pause to wipe off the extra ink after making each line, so you get a little breather in between. And the black outline hurts less than the fill-in color. So I thought, *Well, this is not unbearable.*

And as he got close to finishing, I thought, *Wow, this is daring and exciting.* And I'm cool. (Cher, dream on.)

The whole process took forty-five minutes. After I got home, I went right in to show Son. "Yeah, fine, that's *great,* Cher," he said. He was exasperated with me, like a father with a teenager.

But that butterfly was more than a symbol of rebellion. It was really the first step of an experiment: to start making decisions on my own. I was twenty-seven years old, and I'd seen a lot, but I'd also lived a sheltered life. I'd never gone on an airplane by myself. I'd never been in a bank. I had never done the everyday things that most people didn't give a thought to.

Also, I had made so few real decisions that I was bound to be pretty bad at it. I was right. I *was* bad at it.

My First Evening with a New Friend

For the year and a half we did <u>The Sonny and Cher</u> *Comedy Hour* after our separation, I didn't have much of a social life. That was a deal I made with Sonny, that I wouldn't go out in public without him, because everyone was talking about us already. So we went together to hear Bette Midler at the Troubadour, and to Lou Adler's Christmas party—those were probably the only two places I went, and David Geffen was at both of them.

He was this funny, cute guy, and he had a very quick way about him. So when he asked me to come to his house for dinner, I said, "Sure, that would be great." The only friends I had were Paulette and Joey and my sister, and I thought, *Maybe this could be my first new friend.*

When David gave me his address, I thought it sounded familiar. And when I drove out the next night, I realized that he lived around the block. Which confused me, because I thought for some reason that David was a record-promotion man. I pulled up to this big, beautiful Spanish house, which used to be owned by Julie Andrews, and I wondered, *What the hell is a promotion man doing living here?*

David answered the door with a phone in his hand—"Come in, I didn't have a chance to change." He was wearing a plaid shirt and jeans and loafers, which was what he always wore. We sat down to dinner with Lou Adler, who was there for protection—David thought I might be some sort of carnivore.

Later, after Lou left, I asked David what he did. He said, "I started Elektra/Asylum Records." When I told him what I'd thought he did, he just started laughing.

We ended up telling each other our entire life stories that night. It felt so good to be able to be myself, without watching every word I said. I could trust David from the beginning.

It was late when Joni Mitchell came walking through a door to tell David she was on her way out. After she left, I said, "So what is she doing here?"

David said, "She's recording an album, and she's living with me." (The album was *Court and Spark*.)

I thought, *This is getting stranger and stranger.*

We talked into the early morning. I had just enough time to run home, take a shower and go straight to the studio. David and I had so much fun together. It was like we really knew each other, even though we'd just met. He was kind and giving and shy. He was my new best friend.

When I got to work, Sonny wasn't happy that I'd been out all night. But I was my own person now. Or at least my own semiperson.

Look how sweet Dave looks here.
But what's with the hat, Cher?

The First Man Who Read Me My Rights

David Geffen was a genius at business. He was (and still is) the smartest person I've ever met, and with no effort. If he saw a problem, he solved it—that was just his way. And, of course, I was a bundle of problems; I couldn't find my ass with both hands.

I had assumed that Sonny and I would split everything if for some reason there was no more Sonny and Cher—neither of us had anything when we met, so that made sense to me. But in early 1974, when CBS was about to pick up the show's option for another season, David asked me, "What's your contract? Where does the money go? What do you get paid?"

"I don't know," I said. "I never asked." David said he thought it was time I did.

So I asked for a copy of my contract, and I brought it to David. After he read it, he said, "This contract is ridiculous. Sweetheart, this is just not right. As happy as you are with your little checking account and your rented house at the beach, this contract gives you no rights—no money, and you can't do any work that Cher Enterprises doesn't allow you to do."

According to my contract, I was an employee of Cher Enterprises. Sonny owned 95 percent of the company, and Irwin, our lawyer (great lawyer!), owned the other 5 percent. Every dollar we made went into Cher Enterprises, but I couldn't draw a check on the account unless it was signed by Sonny or Irwin. To make things worse, I was signed exclusively to Cher Enterprises for two more years. I couldn't go out and do performances, or records, or TV, or anything on my own to make money.

I couldn't believe it. I'd heard about this thing called Cher Enterprises forever, but I didn't really know what it was. I went to Son and told him that I wanted to dissolve Cher Enterprises and draw up a new contract between us, one where we would we split everything fifty-fifty. "That way everything would be fair and we could keep doing the show," I said. "And if you don't, I'm not gonna work—even if they pick up the option."

"You'll get sued," Son told me.

"I don't give a damn," I said. "We didn't have shit when we met, Son. Fifty-fifty is fair."

But Son wouldn't do it. He felt he had created Sonny and Cher, and he knew that if we were equal partners, he would lose complete control. I tried to explain that we would still do our work the way we'd always done it, but he wasn't going for it.

He tried to push me and coax me and reason with me, but I wasn't listening. He was pissed, but he was nervous, too, because he knew that David was powerful and smart.

I didn't know what to do; I was afraid to make a move. I didn't want to leave a show I loved doing, and I didn't want to leave Son either. As strange as it sounds, I loved living with Son in the big house, even though he was at one end with Connie, and I was at the other. We all spent time together, we joked, we laughed. Son and I were still family. But I wanted what I felt was fair, and I couldn't go on with Sonny in control of everything in my life. So I called Freddie Silverman at CBS and told him exactly what was happening. Nobody in his right mind would have broken up *The Sonny and Cher Comedy Hour* at that point. But I explained to Freddie that I couldn't go on being an employee of Cher Enterprises. I begged him to talk to Son and, if that failed, to let me go.

And CBS dropped the option.

My First Bad Boy

At the end of 1974, I went to see Gregg Allman perform at the Troubadour, a teeny club in Hollywood. Gregory was sitting in on the piano with some friends, for fun. The Allman Brothers were one of the top rock bands at the time.

During a set, a guy came up to me and gave me a little note, but it was too dark to read it. Later, when my sister and I went to the bathroom, she asked me what the note had said, and I told her, "I don't know. I couldn't read it in the dark." I handed it to her, and she bent down to read it in the light of a cigarette machine. And it said, "Dear lovely lady" (Gregory was so flowery) "I'm not supposed to play here another night, but if you would come back, I would deem it an honor to play for you tomorrow night."

I just thought, *Oh, well. Okay, that's nice.* But I wasn't in a very receptive mood. Still, I felt there was something there between us, so I gave Gregory my number.

He called me the next night and asked me out on a date, which was something I'd never really done before as a grown-up—go out with a complete stranger. It was a fiasco. We went to a party at Edgar Winter's hotel room at the Continental Hyatt, and then to another party at Judy Carne's house, and all I saw were these horrible, drugged-out people. (Why didn't I read the huge, hand-painted signs?)

Then Gregory took me to some restaurant on the Sunset Strip. He talked about taking me to Hawaii. And I thought, *What's with this guy?*

I'm pregnant. It was a car crash waiting to happen.

It's only our first date and already we're going to Hawaii? I wasn't used to being talked to in that way. I was having a terrible time, and finally I told him I wanted to go home.

The next day I was doing a fitting for the *Cher* show, which was about to premiere as a CBS special, and I broke out crying, because the date had been so horrible. I was so backward. I just wasn't any good at dating, and I didn't think I ever would be because I didn't know how to do it.

But that night the telephone rang, and it was Gregory. He said, "That date was so awful. Let's try it again." (Does this make sense to you?) We went to dinner and then dancing at a club in Beverly Hills. We just sat and talked, but it was very different from the night before, because Gregory wasn't trying to impress me this time. He was being himself.

I was naïve about drugs then. I'd never been around anyone with a real problem before (except my father, but I was too young then to truly understand what my mother was having to deal with). When I heard people say he was doing heroin, I'd insist that he wasn't.

Anybody with two eyes could have seen that we were a disaster waiting to happen. I had to have known it was the wrong thing to do, but there was something about Gregory. He was handsome and wild. He was rock 'n' roll—the definitive Bad Boy; he was also tender and sensitive.

I think I was looking for someone who wouldn't try to dominate me. And I never felt that Gregory would try to box me in, because it wasn't in him to put that box together.

Maybe if it hadn't been for all the drugs, things would have ended differently for Gui Gui (Gregory) and me. Maybe not. We were young and so messed up. Bless our cotton socks.

Our Las Vegas wedding. Oh God! I knew I was in trouble. I cried all the way home.

Entering the White House for a reception with President Carter. Gregg and I were invited later for dinner. I would have never thought that I would be having dinner with the President—and on his first night in office.

Our marriage was falling
apart, but I just wouldn't
say uncle.

I'd hoped this album would keep us together; so did Gregory.

My First War with the Censors

With David Geffen producing, the <u>Cher</u> show was a huge success. It knocked off *The Wonderful World of Disney* on Sunday night, which Freddie Silverman and CBS had been trying to do since the year dot.

That didn't help me with the network censors, however. The executives were worried about me because Son and I had always been so wholesome (well, Son was wholesome; I was on the fringe).

On the *Cher* show, I had not just one censor on my set, but two, a man and a woman. And I don't know where they came from, but they interpreted everything as being about sex.

It was the strangest thing. When I was married and doing *The Sonny and Cher Comedy Hour,* I could get away with all kinds of double entendre stuff, and nobody took it seriously. But after my divorce, all that changed. In one skit I was doing on my show, I had to turn to Wayne Rogers and say, "He's my lover."

And the censors said, "You can't say 'lover'—you have to say 'boyfriend.' Because 'lover' implies sex."

They were also constantly objecting to my dresses: either they were cut too low or revealed too much. (Were these censors living in a cave the whole time the *Sonny and Cher Show* was on?) I had a wonderful, all-sequined dress—clear sequins, but you couldn't see anything, because it was all backed. And the censors made our editor do a wipe on it, so that everything just about disappeared in fogginess, even me.

Another time I was doing a song by John Denver, set in a beautiful Paris studio. I was in an amazing bias-cut gown. And the censor came over and said, "She looks like a hooker."

I was in tears. Norman Lear happened to be walking down the

hallway, and I grabbed him and said, "Norman, will you come in here and look at this number and tell me what you think?"

And he came in and watched it, and he said, "It's beautiful."

And I said, "Will you go over and talk to the fucking censors?"

Norman went over and argued the case for me, and we won.

It was all kind of silly, because the thing CBS wanted me on the air for was the very thing they weren't allowing me to do.

The First Time I Got Kissed at Divorce Court

The only way I could get free of my contract with Son was by divorcing him.

We were in court to make the divorce final when for some insane reason known only to the Italian stallion, he decides to prove that I was an unfit mother (you gotta love him). This was just stupid; we both knew it, and I was furious with him. The judge warned his lawyer that they "could be getting into a dangerous area."

We walked out of the courtroom, and Son grabbed me and kissed me on the mouth. He started laughing, then I started laughing—I couldn't help it. It wasn't a game; I don't know exactly what it was. I wanted to be mad at him. I *was* mad at him. But I couldn't stay mad at him; there was this stupid thing between us that I couldn't cut, something in that strange, gray Sonny and Cher zone.

A visit to the Tonight Show. Sonny and I were still close at this point. We talked every day.

The road was tough;
there was just no
getting around that.

Son was always coming
up with crazy ways to
play the piano in the
vamp number.

My First Reunion with Sonny

Once Dave Geffen stopped producing the <u>Cher</u> *show,* it all went to pieces. CBS put on a horrible summer replacement show in my time slot with Joey Heatherton and her father, called *Joey and Dad.* By the time I got back in the fall, I was up against the number-one-rated show, *The Six Million Dollar Man,* which rated last when I'd left. It was a nightmare.

I dreaded doing the monologues, because I was so bad at them, and I got tired of fighting the censors and the producer on my own. Without David there to protect me, I was in way over my head. I wasn't able to have fun with it anymore, which is death for comedy.

So I asked Son to come back with me.

The day we announced the new series, Son and I were sitting in our old bedroom in the Big House. And I said, "Son, I've got something to tell you."

(In our old skits, Son used to shoot me an exasperated look and hit the side of his head, and go, "*Sheesh,* Cher.") Which was exactly what he did when I told him I was pregnant.

The new *Sonny and Cher Show* was a first for American television. I was back working with Son, I was pregnant with someone else's child, and the father, Gregg Allman, was filing for divorce—and Son and I are openly joking about all of it. Nobody had ever seen anything like *that* before on TV; CBS was reeling.

Our second show was as funny, if not funnier, than the original. Son and I were still great together, even if the barbs had a different meaning. But people didn't like it. They loved Sonny and Cher when *we* were in love and happy.

With Elton John, Flip Wilson, and Bette Midler. Flip walked out in the middle of taping. He never came back.

There was a real panther on this set, and my hair was tied to a f———g tree!

My First Run-In with Elijah

My son was less than nine months old when we went to Hawaii and rented a house there. We were hanging out in the backyard, by the swimming pool, when Elijah crawled over to the water meter, which was recessed a few inches into the ground. There were all kinds of weeds and wet leaves and other stuff in it—it was kind of gross. When Elijah started playing with it, I went over and said, "No, Elijah, it's dirty."

A minute or two later, I saw him over there again, playing with the meter. And I said, "Elijah, this is dirty! This is awful! There are bugs in there, yech! We gotta wash your hands."

I sat back down, but this time I watched him. Elijah crawled around in front of the water meter, looking straight at me, and then he stuck his hand behind his back and put it into all that wet slimy junk again.

I thought, *Oh, shit.* I could not believe it. I smacked his hand and said, "Elijah, it's *dirty.* It's *ca-ca.* Don't play in it!"

I sat back down and waited. This time he crawled around the other way and stuck his other hand behind him. I picked him up and popped his butt. He glared at me, tears shooting out of his eyes. He was furious.

Who's the cutest boy in the world?

When I put him down, he crawled out to the back gate and opened it; he was eight months old, and he was running (well, crawling) away from home.

I was in deep trouble.

My First Solo Club Act

By 1978, I was a working single parent with two children and loads of debt. I had to go back to the clubs, and this time on my own.

When my first show opened at the Sahara Reno, we were so far behind schedule that we didn't even get a dress rehearsal. There were a thousand people out there, and everything was breaking down. I kept thinking, *This is insane. You're not gonna be able to do this. Oh my God, oh my God.*

Thank God I had my old friend Laverne to open the show.

Laverne was born on *The Sonny and Cher Comedy Hour,* and she was the only character I ever created—sort of an Edith Bunker meets Lucille Ball. She was a bizarre woman with a big, fat stomach and little squeaky legs, and red hair with black roots. And she always wore the same outfit, which Bob Mackie and Ret Turner and I put together: a tiger-skin jumpsuit, and those awful high heels that women in Florida put dice or goldfish in, and pink earrings the size of Ping-Pong balls.

When we first tried Laverne out, in a skit for a studio audience, I had everything down but her voice. I'd tried several different ones, but none of them was right. I was standing there, ready to go on, but knowing I didn't quite have her yet.

Then one of the grips on the set came up and asked me if I wanted some bubblegum. "Yeah," I said. "Gimme two pieces." And I walked onstage, chewing, and Laverne was born. The gum brought her to life.

That first night in Reno, everybody was expecting Cher—and that's when Laverne came through the audience. People loved it; the ice was broken. After a short sketch, I went backstage, and they pulled off my costume. I came right back on and started to sing, and the fire alarm went off. I was stunned, but I looked at the audience and said, "I know

I'm hot, but this is ridiculous." Then I started to sing again, and in the middle of my first song, we lost sound. All the power in the place was down. It was a nightmare (like when you dream you're in school and suddenly your teacher gives a test and you haven't studied for it).

I was almost paralyzed, but, out of nowhere, I thought fast on my feet and said, "I knew Sonny was gonna come in here and screw it up." Everybody started to laugh, and the show went well from then on. Even though it wasn't perfect, it had a *feeling*. And if you can create a feeling, nothing else really matters.

That was one of the million things Son taught me. ⟿

My First Show at Caesar's

When I got a contract with Caesar's Palace, Las Vegas was much less developed than it is now. Nothing else compared to Caesar's—it was the biggest club in the country. I saw Frank Sinatra there the night before I opened, and it was hard to believe that I was about to go up on that same stage.

By that point I knew pretty much what I was doing onstage. I'd been frightened to build a show just around me, so there were a lot of other elements. We started with a taped segment, from my baby pictures to film clips of Sonny and myself and Chastity and Elijah. Then I walked through these slits in the screen, in a Bob Mackie gown, and we were off.

At Caesar's we introduced J.C. Gaynor and Kenny Sasha, two unbelievable drag queens. (I guess now it's improper to use that term, but J.C. and Kenny were great female impersonators. The best I ever saw was Elgin Kenna. He's Drag Queen of the Universe.) I'd be about to start a number, when I'd hear a voice from offstage—Diana Ross's voice—going, "Cher?"

And I'd say, "Diana, is that you?"

It was Diana Ross. But what the audience didn't know is that we'd gotten Diana to tape a few lines for us, and then we'd used the tape to work out a dialogue onstage between Diana and me that sounded perfectly natural.

After some more back-and-forth talk, Diana would say, "Well, I'm coming right out—I'm on my way!" And J.C. would come onstage in an exact replica of one of Diana's gowns, and lip-synch to "Ain't No Mountain High Enough." After he took his bow, I'd come back out to give him a kiss, and then Kenny would come onstage (dressed as Bette Midler) and lip-synch to "Boogie-Woogie Bugle Boy."

As a finish, the three of us did a version of "Friends," and the audience would go wild. People weren't used to drag queens in those days, and they actually thought they were seeing Diana Ross, Bette Midler, and Cher onstage together. They never knew what was going on. Even when I introduced J.C. and Kenny at the end of the show as themselves, they didn't get much applause, because the audience had no idea what they'd done in the show. People just didn't get it.

The First Time I Knew I Was Dyslexic

When Chas was ten years old, she wasn't doing well in school, so I was called in to meet with the principal. Everything this woman said was negative and scary. She was sure that my daughter had emotional problems by the way she was doing her homework, and that I should get Chas to a doctor. I left her office crying.

"That's bullshit," said Betsy Glaser, Chas's teacher, who'd been in on the meeting. "Don't believe it for a second. Chas is smart, but I think she has some sort of learning problem. You've got to have her evaluated."

I took Chas to a top testing center in Los Angeles, and that's when I found out that she was dyslexic. The doctors also asked me about my own reading and writing. I told them how my mind raced ahead of my hand, how I'd skip letters in the middle of a word. I told them how I kept transposing numbers, and that I'd get so cranky trying to dial long-distance calls that someone would finally have to take the phone and dial the number for me.

They told me that I was dyslexic, too. It was like a big, *Ohhh.* . . . Now I understood everything, why I had so much trouble with school. It all fit together.

Up till then, I never wrote letters, not even a postcard, because I was so embarrassed about my spelling. But now I didn't care so much, and I actually got some pen pals: Paddy Chayevsky, Henry Kissinger, Michael Korda. I told them upfront that I couldn't spell, and to let me know if it was a problem. I guess it wasn't.

My First Name

When I was married to Sonny, I was Cher Bono. When I was married to Gregory, I was Cher Allman. After my second divorce, I settled on Cher Bono Allman, because I didn't want either of my children to feel left out.

One day I woke up and thought: *Screw this—I don't want either one of these names.*

So I petitioned the court to legally change my name to Cher, with no last name at all. It isn't an easy thing to do. You have to prove that everyone would know who you are by just hearing the one name and that you couldn't possibly be confused with anyone else.

When the court approved my petition, I had the change made on my passport, my driver's license, everything. It just felt right to me. From the time I was little, I was always just Cher. (Or what the kids in my road show called me: "J. P. C.," or "Just Plain Cher.")

It didn't always work on the phone, however. When I'd call someone I didn't know, I'd say, "Hi, this is Cher." And they'd say, "Who?" And then I'd have to say, "Cher, of Sonny and Cher." That always worked.

I had to do that for the longest time.

The First Time I Went for Broke

I was making a fortune on the road. But I was dying inside. Everyone kept saying, "Cher, there are people who would give anything to have standing room only at Caesar's Palace. It would be the pinnacle of their careers." And I kept thinking, *Yes, I should be satisfied, I've got to be satisfied.*

But I wasn't satisfied.

One night Francis Ford Coppola came backstage after catching my show. "You're so good," he said. "Why aren't you doing movies?"

I tried to keep the tears back. I'd been trying to get a job in movies since Elijah was born, and now he was five years old. It wasn't that people didn't know me. I hung out with Jack Nicholson and Anjelica Huston and Warren Beatty. I went to directors and producers in New York and California, and I couldn't get arrested.

I was getting fed up with all of these studio guys and the crap they were telling me. I was either too old or too tall or too ethnic, or "Cher" would look too stupid on a marquee. There was always some reason it wouldn't work out.

I'd already done a lot—recordings, television, nightclubs—but people were convinced that I couldn't do anything else. I was a singer, a personality—how could I be an actress? Hollywood isn't comfortable with new ideas. They like to lock you into a box so they don't have to think about you anymore. You're a type, not a person.

A lot of movie people said I wasn't "serious" enough. If you're too flamboyant, and you perform in gowns cut down too low or up too high, or you show your navel, people assume that you're an idiot. I guess I needed to be grumpier, or stiffer, or wear more brown tweed. I remember someone actually saying, "If you're going to be a real actress, *you've got to get yourself a last name.*"

I knew that I'd said and done really stupid things on impulse. (And still do.) I didn't weigh upsides and downsides. I had the stigma of being "Cher," of not being serious, and it scared people away. The weird thing was that I'm one of the most morosely serious people I know, even if it doesn't show.

But there comes a time in your life when, if you're going to move forward, you must stop taking no for an answer. Penny Marshall once told me something that stuck in my head. She was walking down the street with Paul Simon at a time when her TV show was a monster hit. Everybody was coming up to her and saying, "Hey, Laverne!" or "I *love Laverne and Shirley!*" And blah-blah-blah-blah-blah.

Just two people came up to Paul Simon, and said to him, "Your music has meant so much to my life." Penny said she was jealous, because even though Paul was affecting fewer people that day, he was affecting them more deeply.

That's what I wanted to do. I'd been famous my whole life, a *celebrity* (a word I hated). I didn't care about being famous anymore; I wanted to be *good.* I wanted to touch people deeply.

Then I did a TV special with Shelley Winters. She told me, "If you're serious about acting, go to New York. Don't fuck around and talk about it—just do it." I knew she was right. I also knew that time was running out. I was thirty-five years old, an age when most actresses begin to wind down. If I was going to start, it was now or never.

So as soon as my house was built and partially paid for, I left Los Angeles. (L.A. is kind of like heroin—it feels lovely and peaceful, and then it kills you.) I left my high-roller suite behind me, and I moved to the other end of the world: New York. I had no real confidence or faith that I'd succeed there. I did it with willpower. There was nothing else for me to do. ⟳

He was so happy about his Palm Springs restaurant.
And I'm still in my stupid braces.

My First Acting Breakthrough

A month or so before I was supposed to start studying with Lee Strasberg, I auditioned for Joe Papp, on the off chance that I might get into one of his Public Theater productions. (I'd just seen Linda Ronstadt in *Pirates of Penzance.)*

When we returned to his office, Joe's receptionist had a message for me on one of those little slips of while-you-were-out paper: "Please call Robert Altman." I thought, *O my God, I've gone from nobody to* two *bodies.*

What had happened was this: My mother was trying to reach me at Joe's office, to find out how my audition had gone, and had dialed her old friend Kathryn Altman by mistake. She woke Bob up from a nap and asked if I was there.

Which got Bob real crabby, and he said, "What the hell would Cher be doing here?" After they sorted things out, and he realized who was who, my mom told Bob what I was doing in New York, and he asked how he could reach me. I called him back immediately.

Bob said, "Look, I've got a script for a play I'm doing on Broadway, and I'm going to send it over. I want you to read it."

As soon as I started reading *Come Back to the Five & Dime, Jimmy Dean, Jimmy Dean,* I knew that Bob would see me as Joe, the transsexual. It was the obvious part for me, but I didn't want to do it, because I didn't think I could do a good job of it. I wanted to play Sissy, the small-town sexpot who'd secretly had a double mastectomy. She might not seem as good a match for me on the surface, but I understood her completely.

I told Bob what I thought. I wasn't thinking about diplomacy, or the fact that I had no experience, or that someone should have been ripping the tongue out of my mouth. And Bob said, "Well, we already have someone to play Sissy." When I stayed firm, he said, "Let's not get too entrenched here. Let's both be open. Come on over and we'll talk—a couple of the girls will be here."

(Someone please slap me. Who the fuck do I think I am, talking to Robert Altman that way?)

I threw on my leather jacket and went to this beautiful apartment building on Central Park South. A little older woman got into the elevator with me and pressed my same floor. I got off right behind her and followed her to Bob's door—it was Sudie Bond. (She later told me she thought I was going to mug her.)

When I stepped inside, I saw Kathy Bates and Sandy Dennis and Karen Black. They were sitting on the floor, and I didn't know any of them. They were chitchatting about people they knew and work they'd done, and I felt completely out of place.

I thought we'd come just to talk, or do whatever theater people do when they get together. But then Bob brought out the scripts, and I went numb. We were going to *read*. I was never any good at readings; I couldn't focus on a whole sentence at once and make sense of it. But Bob said, "Oh, come on. I just want to hear how your voices sound together."

We all read different parts. I read Sissy a lot better than I read Joe; I had a feeling for Sissy. But it was a disaster, either way.

Sandy told me later, after we got to be good friends, that that first reading at Bob's apartment was without a doubt the worst audition she'd ever witnessed. "You were fascinating," she said. "I could not take my eyes off you. It was like looking at a train wreck. That's just how bad you were."

But Bob must have seen something he liked. After we finished reading, he asked me to stay behind, and then he asked what I thought about his films. I said I loved most of them, but I thought he had ruined *Popeye*, because It was "too dark in spirit, and you couldn't understand what Robin Williams was saying." (Why doesn't someone stop me. Just put a muzzle over my mouth.)

Bob didn't seem offended, although it's hard to know with him. He said, "So what's the problem with Joe?"

I said, "I just think I'd be a better Sissy."

Bob said, "Well, you're right. You weren't very good as Joe. You're right for Sissy." Then he told me I had to be back on such-and-such a date.

"What does this mean?" I said.

And he said, "It means that you need to be back here on that date so we can start rehearsals."

I was amazed. Actually, I was flabbergasted. (My mouth was finally shut!) I'd had this dramatic vision of studying with Lee Strasberg, giving up everything to learn about the Method, and then finding a job. But it all happened backwards; I got a job before I had a chance to get the Method.

I called my agents at William Morris because I wasn't a member of Actors Equity and needed to find out how you got into the union. I started to explain, "I need some information about *Come Back to the Five & Dime*—"

"Oh, I'm sorry," the agent said, "This play is very serious. Robert Altman is only reading the top people. We couldn't possibly get you an audition."

I said, "You don't have to get me an audition—I already got the part. I just want to know how to get into Equity." I thought, *Ooh, you guys are such assholes. . . .*

It didn't bother me that I was starting my acting career on Broadway. If you're going to be an artist, and you're going to have a chance to be great, you have to risk looking foolish in high places sometimes. You have to paint a big target on your ass and go, *All right, everybody, step right up. Here it is—take your best shot.*

My First Opening Night

We'd been in previews for <u>Jimmy Dean</u> for three weeks and had to turn people away every night. I was having a ball, so I thought this acting thing was a cinch. It was a game where all the players were on the same team. Sandy Dennis was so great and funny and giving as an actress—she even gave me Elizabeth Taylor's old dressing room. (Which might have been the only nice one on Broadway.)

This is perfect, I thought. I went to the theater and did my thing. Then I went dancing at Studio 54, or hung out with my friends at Café Central. Bruce Willis was a bartender there and I once gave Johnny Goodman a peptalk and money for a beer. Life was good.

We opened on February 18, 1982, at the Martin Beck Theatre, and that night I had a massive attack of stage fright right before intermission. I was doing a scene with Sandy, who was standing by the cash register—and I looked up and I *saw* her for the very first time. And I thought, *I'm on Broadway, I have Elizabeth Taylor's dressing room, and I'm onstage with Sandy Dennis who's won an Oscar . . . Shit!*

Then the most horrible wave of fear ran through my body and I shook. I couldn't catch my breath; I was paralyzed. As soon as the curtain fell, I ran back to Sandy's dressing room and told her I didn't think I could go back on—I just couldn't do it. And she said, "Why don't you just try it for a little while, and then you can decide. Don't worry, you'll get through this."

I had to force myself to go onstage for the second act and not to run off once I got there. My heart was pounding, my face was sweating. But the second half of *Jimmy Dean* was where my part of the roller coaster took off, and I didn't have time to think about how scared I was . . . Suddenly the lights went black, and then we were taking our bows.

As we got into our run, there were nights when I knew that I sucked. But there were also other nights like that first one, where I'd get so into the performance that I didn't even remember it as a performance. It would be like fainting and waking up to applause. Those were the nights when I knew I was really good. But it wasn't a cinch.

My First Born-Again Production

The reviewers did their best to kill <u>Jimmy Dean</u>.
Frank Rich called our play a "dreary amateur night." *Variety* said it was "preposterous, undramatic, and silly." Rex Reed called it "a confusing, trivial, and completely contrived piece of chicken-fried silliness."

Still, I had no idea that a huge ax was about to fall. I didn't think that a few bad notices would make such a difference. Of course I was wrong.

It's a weird thing, the power of theater reviews. A play can be selling out in previews, with standing ovations every night. Then one night goes by that really isn't any different from the night before, and the house is only half full, and everyone's saying how sorry they are for you. That's what happened to us, and it was frightening. When you get bad reviews, the producers stop paying for advertising and promotion. They want to cut their losses and let it end. That's why some shows shut down within a week.

We were down so low after our opening night. People expected us to close right away, but that's when Bob Altman decided to put his own money into the play. Slowly, through word of mouth, we built *Jimmy Dean* back up. I remember the first good night we had was when a gay group bought up all the tickets. The play was sensational that night, and these guys loved it—they gave us so much back.

We got our confidence back that night, and we ended up the run having great audiences. Standing room only, some nights. They were also very strange groups, from little blue-haired ladies at our matinees, to outrageous theatrical-looking people, to regulars who came back again and again. I started noticing people wearing sweatshirts with our logo; a girl named Cheryl was selling them on her own outside the theater, and she gave one to everyone in the cast. In sixty performances, we built a little subculture. ⟶⟜

The First Time I Had to Fight for My Ad Libs

Sissy was a complex character from the start, but as I got closer to her, I got better at making her funny, taking her further and further away from where I knew she had to go to at the end of the play. As the run went on, I could find Sissy in any of the houses she lived in—the tough woman, the hilarious woman, the hurt woman. Even at her funniest moments, I could never forget about Sissy's secret, or pretend that it didn't exist, because that would be tricking the audience, cheating them.

Before we started, I worried that my performance would get stale after a while. But when words go from paper to life, they come out in a new way each time. It's not something an actor plans; it just happens. (On the last night of our run, one of my lines came out kind of backwards, and I thought, *So that's what that line meant.*)

And then there were nights when the dialogue wasn't exactly the same. I didn't know that you weren't supposed to ad lib on Broadway. If I thought of something different than my line in the script, I said it. Bob seemed to be fine with that. Nothing ruffled Sandy Dennis, who could catch anything you threw at her and throw it right back. Karen Black and I never got along anyway, in our roles or anything else, but she could definitely think on her feet and stand toe to toe with you.

One person who had a problem with my ad libs was the writer (Duh—no kidding, Cher). Ed Graczyk didn't want me changing his words. He had every right to be upset; I just didn't know the rules. We were still in rehearsal when he went to Bob and complained. Bob came to me and said, "Cher, I want you to learn that script and I want you to learn it now, verbatim." He could be a gruff old bear, and he was pissed off.

So I learned the script, and then we gave a preview performance, and I followed my lines to the letter. But Ed still found something I wasn't saying right, and Bob came up and started growling at me. And I said, "I did it verbatim. You heard me—you were there."

And then Bob said, "I've never actually read it all the way through." Which got me laughing hysterically.

After we opened, and my ad libs got laughs, Bob changed his mind: "You say whatever's funniest." Even Ed said it was okay with him. After that, Ed and I became pretty tight. I would have stayed pissed if I were him. ⁓

The First Time a Sandwich
Got Me in Trouble

<u>Jimmy Dean</u> was so much fun for me. It was like a vacation to be able to hide behind a character. In a play, you get people to watch you by pretending they're not there. You never have to look at them, or wait for them to clap. I felt so comfortable and safe with the other women in the cast that when the curtain opened, I felt like I was slipping into a warm bathtub.

Once I got into trouble for being too free. There's a point in the play where I'm just making sandwiches. They weren't flashy sandwiches—cheese and bologna on white bread with mayonnaise—but I really got into making them. Some of the girls, I never knew who, complained to Bob and said that I was "too alive" onstage. And Sandy said, "Fuck them. You just keep making your little sandwiches."

One night everyone was talking about what they did to prepare before going on stage. Some people did breathing exercises. Some looked over their material for the thousandth time. Some went to vomit. (And I thought *I* was terrified.)

When they got to me, I said, "What I do to prepare is make sure I don't get to the theater too early." They all looked at me like I was crazy, but it was true. I only got frightened when I had extra time to think about things.

Not that all of my performances were great. When you do eight shows a week, there are nights that you think you suck. You want to commit suicide. One night I wasn't able to cry in my big scene, and I went to Sandy and said, "I'm not *good* every night."

And she said, "Am I supposed to feel sorry for you? If you're *brilliant,* you'll be good three nights a week." She was right, though I didn't want to believe her. I so wanted to be brilliant *every* night. . . .

The miraculous thing about theater is that even when you're horrible, you can redeem yourself the next night. And even when you're great, you can only electrify an audience for a finite piece of time. You've got to catch the moment, because soon it will be over, and it will never happen in that same way again. That's what makes the theater magical, and that's what I loved about it. ~⌒

My First Real Movie Offer

When I played on Broadway, matinees were my specialty.
The other girls in *Jimmy Dean* didn't like them as much because the ladies who came were just taking in a play after lunch or shopping. But I didn't care about that. I loved the freedom of matinees. I could experiment without feeling pressured.

On one particular Wednesday afternoon, I think I was the best I ever was in *Jimmy Dean.* After we got off the stage, everybody came rushing up to me: "You were so good today! What happened?"

Two minutes after I reached my dressing room, there was a knock on the door. I never wanted to be told who was in the audience—I didn't want to know until it was over. I had no idea that Mike Nichols had snuck into the matinee, and now there he was.

Years before, I'd met with Mike to talk about a part in *The Fortune,* and he had said no to me. And I said to him, "You know what? I am talented, and one day you are going to be so sorry." And I walked out of his office in a huff.

Now Mike was in my dressing room, and he said, "You were right— you *are* talented." And then he said, "Do you want to make a movie with me and Meryl Streep?"

I'm not sure which I lost first, my hearing or my vision. Somehow I managed to say something like, "Sure."

"Do you want to know what it's about?"

"I don't care," I said.

The movie was *Silkwood.* A couple of weeks after Mike saw me backstage, he called me again and said, "I just want to tell you that your character is a lesbian, but she's a *lovely* lesbian."

"Okay, fine," I said. "It doesn't make any difference to me."

After we filmed *Come Back to the Five & Dime, Jimmy Dean, Jimmy*

Dean, I went back home to L.A., and for a while I was two feet off the ground. It was only when I began packing to go to Dallas and start the film that I realized how ridiculous this was. I started unpacking.

My sister was with me, and she said, "What's the matter?"

"I can't go," I said. "I can't go and make a movie with Meryl Streep." I had seen *The Deer Hunter* and *Kramer vs. Kramer,* and I thought there was no actress working who compared with Meryl. No one else wore their characters like a second skin, made them so completely alive. She was simply better than everybody else—and how could I possibly share the same screen with her?

Georganne was putting my clothes back in the bags while I was taking them out. She tried to reason with me: "If they didn't want you, they wouldn't have asked you."

"I know that, but what am I going to do when I get there? I'm not good enough to act with her."

And my sister said, "They *want* you. Just *go.*" So I went, scared to death, but I went.

I was sweating bullets when I walked into the production office to meet Meryl. Then I saw this glowing apparition stand up and float toward me: white hair, white eyebrows, white dress. It was Meryl, who'd colored her hair for *Sophie's Choice.* She held out her arms and said, "Oh, I'm so glad that you're here." She gave me a huge hug.

My First Job as a Stable Girl

Dolly Pelliker was a composite of Karen Silkwood's sister and Karen's friend. At the beginning, she was written as this glamorous barrel rider. We tried a screen test of Dolly that way, and Mike Nichols just didn't like it. A day or two later, while we were hanging out in the house that our characters lived in for the movie, Mike came in with Annie Ross, our costume designer, and a rack of clothes.

"We're going to try something," Mike said. "Go wash your face, and take your hair and wet it, and then let it dry flat to your head." I did as I was told. "Okay, now put on these clothes." I went in and changed, but Mike and Annie weren't satisfied; they said I still looked like a *Vogue* model. They were just merciless with me, until I had on some horrible men's bowling shirt and awful chino pants, with two pairs of jockey shorts underneath to make me look heavier. My pants were too short and my sleeves were too long—everything was off, one way or the other.

When I stepped out in my new costume, Kurt Russell said, "What the fuck are *you* supposed to be?" I ran in tears to the back bathroom, which had the only mirror in the house. And I cried my eyes out.

The director of photography for *Silkwood* was a Czech named Mirac Ondricek, and he had yet to acknowledge that I was alive. But when he heard me crying in the bathroom, Mirac came in and tapped me with his cane, and he said, "Darling, it's the *ice*" (he was talking about my eyes). "The ice is beautiful. Don't care about anything else—the ice is *beautiful*."

But I was looking at the big picture. Everyone was trying not to laugh and not doing a very good job of it. Mike was looking really pleased. "That's perfect," he said.

I couldn't believe it. My first real time in front of a camera in a big film, and *this* was the way I had to look?

It was hard on me to see Meryl and Kurtie with makeup and hair people all over them and be totally ignored. Mike would give me the white-glove test; he'd run his finger across my cheek, to make sure I hadn't snuck on a touch of something. Once I tried to cheat and curled my eyelashes, and Mike said, "Don't do it again, my dear." He said it sweetly, but I got the message.

Eventually I gave up and got into the spirit of the game. I thought of Dolly as one of those women who works in a stable. She has no preoccupation with her physical self, her hair, or her makeup. She's kind of funny, but she doesn't know it; she's a female version of a good ol' boy.

Before long it became a godsend not to have to worry about how I looked. My whole life I had been consumed with my appearance, but now I was free of it, like a child is free. If I was late, I could roll out of bed straight onto the set, without a glance in a mirror. Since all my clothes were bad, there was never a morning when I thought, *Oh, I'm gonna look good today.* I had one sweatshirt and a pair of pants that passed for my good clothes. That was as close to cute as I got.

You can't play a character as a lesbian. You have to play her as a woman. When Dolly had her relationship with the Diana Scarwid character, she was like an awkward adolescent—and it was her awkwardness that mattered, not her orientation. There are only a few feelings, anyway, and it doesn't make any difference what they're cloaked in. ～ơ

The First Time I Had Twenty Too Many Doughnuts

The _Silkwood_ crew would be thrilled on days when I worked, because the movie was so heavy, and I was the comic relief. I had all of the script's light moments and added one or two on my own. Also, I loved to joke around with everyone. I was just happy to be there. One morning I was hungry, so I talked the prop man into having Dolly eat an Entenmann's chocolate doughnut while she sat on the front porch. When Mike saw what I had finagled, he said, "You think this is fun now, but you're going to be sorry."

Kurt Russell told me the same thing. (Kurtie was like a bossy big brother, and I adored him.)

We had to do twenty takes of that porch scene—masters and close-ups and over-your-shoulders—and I had to start on a new doughnut each time. It was like a bad scene out of _Groundhog Day_. Four hours later, I had eaten half or more of two dozen Entenmann's chocolate doughnuts, and I was ready to puke.

But it didn't stop me from loving them to this day. ⟶

This swing was the beginning for me, but look who was pushing it. No one touches her.

My First Sibyl

To me, Meryl Streep was like a sibyl, the woman that the ancient Greeks and Romans went to for wisdom and prophecies. I remember asking her, "What is the most important thing you can tell me about acting?"

"There are two things," she said. "Always work harder in the other person's close-up than you do in your own."

"And what's the second thing?"

And Meryl said, without cracking a smile, "Never work with R——."

There is no one more generous than Meryl when she's acting with you. She has a truly collaborative spirit, which creates a great atmosphere on the set. I knew that she wanted me to be as good in our scenes in *Silkwood* as she was—that's such an important attitude. I try to live up to her example.

Silkwood was a long shoot for me, because I had to be there from beginning to end, and I wasn't in that many scenes. Meryl and I were together constantly for four months. We worked six days a week, and on Sundays we had a little ritual. We'd drive out toward Dallas and stop at the black-eyed-pea restaurant for lunch. Then we'd go to two movies—we saw all the movies we could see. We even went to the first *Rambo* movie, which we thought was stupid. Meryl christened it, *Mommy, He Hit Me First,* and that's how I'll always think of it.

The First Time I Got Tricked into Crying

Mike Nichols never told you how to act; he'd play little tricks on you instead. When Meryl Streep and I were having a fight scene in *Silkwood,* he wouldn't allow us to see each other or communicate the entire day we were shooting it. We had to stay at the opposite ends of the house where the scene took place.

Mike would also tell you little stories about your character. Meryl and I had a scene together on the porch, where we consoled each other after we'd had a huge fight and everything had gone to shit. The two of us were just sitting there one day, waiting for lighting. And Mike started telling us this terribly sad story about the real Karen Silkwood, when she was sick and completely isolated and alone.

Mike is one of the great storytellers of all time, and he made this story so sad that tears were starting to well up in his eyes. He made it so gut-wrenching that Meryl and I were starting to cry ourselves.

Then Mike said: "Action!" He is definitely the best of the best.

Mike was one of the people I always wanted to impress with my takes. He called me "Child," and I called him "Dad"—how I wished that was the truth.

My First Preview of Coming Attractions

A few weeks before <u>Silkwood</u> opened, Mike Nichols called me and said, "The trailer's running in Westwood. Go see it— it's great."

My sister and my manager and I ran out to this theater. There was a Tom Cruise movie playing. The house was full, and it sounds strange, but it hadn't occurred to us that anyone else would actually be there when we came to watch the trailer. We sat down; we were so thrilled. Meryl Streep's name came up on the screen, and everyone went, *"Ooohh. . . ."*

Kurt Russell. *"Ahhhh. . . ."*

And then "Cher" came up—and everyone in the theater started laughing.

My sister started to cry. My manager started to cry. I bit the inside of my cheek, and I thought, *They're all doing it, so it must be organic, like a reflex.* I detached myself from the laughter. I refused to take it personally. It's like what they say in the Mafia—it's just business.

But deep inside, I cracked and broke into a million pieces, like the coyote in the Road Runner cartoons.

My First Oscar Nomination

We got up early to watch the six o'clock news, when the Oscar nominations were announced. When they said my name—for supporting actress, *Silkwood*—my sister was screaming. My manager was screaming. The phone started ringing off the hook.

Everywhere I went, people were congratulating me: "This is so great. This is so fabulous. You're so lucky. You were so good."

But I knew in the back of my head that I was up against a once-in-a-lifetime kind of performance. When I saw *The Year of Living Dangerously,* before there'd been any press about it, I thought the man who played the cameraman was so strange. I'd thrown my program on the floor, and I scrambled for the thing in the dark, to try to see who it was. And then I realized, *That man's not a man. That man's a woman. This is amazing.*

At that point, I wouldn't have dreamed that Linda Hunt and I would be in competition that year.

I had to go to the Oscars with braces on my teeth—it took me five years to straighten them, because I had to keep taking the braces off when I was working. I was dressed to the max, and of course everyone dissed my dress. B.F.D.

The whole thing seemed unreal. It builds up for months, and you go to all the big parties the nights before, and people are going, "Oh, you're a nominee, you're a nominee," and then you go to the Academy Awards, and you're a *nominee. . . .*

And you're hoping, hoping, hoping—and then you hear someone else's name, and you go from a *nominee* to a *loser.* You sit there really embarrassed, and you just want to hide, because everyone's saying, "Oh, I'm so sorry."

Supporting actress is one of the first big awards that they give out.

You have to sit through the rest of the show, and you better be smiling and laughing, because God knows they're going to be panning onto your face. I was self-conscious about my braces anyway. All I wanted to do was sneak out of the building.

After it was over, there was a big space around me—a lot of people were shying away. They didn't know what to say. Then there were the ones who would come up and say, "I'm so sad you didn't win, but I voted for you."

If everyone who said they voted for me had really voted for me, I would have won.

The First Time Chas Drew the Line

Once, when Chas was about fourteen years old, I did something that finally pushed her over the mother/daughter edge. (I'm sure I did a million and one things that pushed her over that particular edge, but this is the one that comes to mind first.)

One day Chas walked in while I was watching TV in my room. It was a show about punk kids in London who were dressed all crazy and had these great Mohawk hairdos. I got up and I said, "Boy, I love that hairstyle. I'm going to get one!"

Chas panicked, locked the door and threw herself against it. She crossed her arms and said, "Mom, you can *not* get a Mohawk! People will think you've lost your mind. You're too old to get a Mohawk, Mom. I won't let you do it!"

At this point she stopped in midsentence, and we just stood there staring at each other for what seemed like an eternity. Then she said, "This is ridiculous. Don't you realize that *you're* the one who's supposed to be barring the door so *I* won't go get a Mohawk?"

We both started laughing hysterically, and I never got my Mohawk that day . . . I got it later! ⌐◯

My First Date with Captain Queeg

I first met Peter Bogdanovich in 1966, when he did a profile of Sonny and me for *The Saturday Evening Post.* In that article, he completely betrayed us, but he trashed me in particular.

But when he directed me in *Mask,* all that could have been water under the bridge. But it wasn't because he was *still* the same man who had written that horrible article about us so many years ago.

The really weird thing about Peter choosing to direct this film was that he hated bikers—including the ones he hired for the movie. He hated who they were and what they represented—not as a director, but as Peter Bogdanovich. He was also allergic to women with any edge to them, especially me. Once we started the movie, he just didn't like me. I was very close to my character, and Rusty Dennis was a tough woman who didn't apologize for anything. Peter confused my character with me.

One day he asked where I wanted to play a scene, and I said, "I think it would be great to do it in the dining room."

And he said, "I think it would be better to do it in the kitchen."

And I said, "Well, then why'd you ask me where I wanted to do it?"

He said, "Well, do you really think it's better in the dining room?"

I said, "Yes, I do."

And he said, "All right," and we did it in the dining room.

But he must have wrestled with himself all night, and thought he'd been pushed around by letting me choose where to do the scene, because the next day he came into my trailer eating a fried egg sandwich and said, "Cher, I just want you to know one thing. This movie isn't about the mother, it's about the boy, and I can cut you out of it."

He unloaded on me, and then said, "Okay, I think this has been a good productive talk"—and he walked out. I was left there, buttoning my blouse and sobbing. When I walked on the set, I was seeing red. At first Peter had no idea that I was upset, but then he realized that he'd done something terribly wrong. When at one point he came over and put his hand on my arm, and it turned to iron. I told him, "Don't *touch* me. I'll do what you want me to do, but do not touch me." I was livid.

Once, on the weekend, I brought my mother to hear me rehearse a song for the soundtrack. It was on my own time, extra work for no pay; it was supposed to be a very informal rehearsal at his house. We walked through his front door, and Peter started yelling at me and my mother in front of everybody: how *dare* I bring my mother! He almost lost his mind—it was like Captain Queeg and the fucking strawberries. He was yelling so much that everyone got freaked. The atmosphere was in a tailspin, so I bailed him out and tried to make everything okay so we were able to continue with the rehearsal.

Peter always wanted me to say my lines the way he acted them out for me. I thought he was wrong, and I'd tell him, even though I was really nervous about it at the beginning. Sometimes I thought I was crazy. I respected Peter's movies—and what did I know, after all? I kept thinking, *You are making a huge mistake, Cher. He's a veteran director, and you have to follow the things he says. Stop doing this.* But if you feel in your guts that someone is telling you to go against your character, you've got to be true to your beliefs and fight for them. When I act, I've got to start with myself, unless I've got a director that I trust.

Nobody else would disagree with Peter, except for Sam Elliott, and Peter was afraid of Sam.

As the shooting went on, I just stopped listening to Peter. We got into constant arguments. One time when he was yelling at me, I was ready to lose it, and Sam stepped in between us. He said to Peter, "You know what, I think it's time to leave her alone for a minute."

And then Eric Stoltz, who played my son, Rocky, said to me, "Ma, you're doing it wrong. When he tells you something, you just go, 'Yes, yes, yes,' and then you do it your way, and he never notices. Watch me."

I watched, and that was exactly what Eric did, and he was right.

*On the set of <u>Mask</u> with Peter Bogdanovich and Sam Elliot.
No matter how I felt about Peter personally, he made one
un . . . believable movie! I owe him big time. And, how cool is Sam.*

And I thought, okay, I could do that. I started saying "Yes, yes, yes," and Peter never noticed.

After they started putting the movie together, and Peter looked at the first assemblages, he stopped giving me line readings. He was actually starting to be nice to me.

When *Mask* came out, I won the Cannes Film Festival award for best actress that year. I was elated, not only for winning the award but also for the people I met there. June Allyson actually knew who I was, and Van Johnson joked around with me! And Jimmy Stewart, one of my idols, won on the same night—which fell on our birthday, May 20. I felt proud to be on the stage with him.

At Cannes, Peter had a big feud with the producer because a scene he liked was cut, and also because they had to substitute a Bob Seger song for a Bruce Springsteen song. He was going to try to take his name off the credits, which is death for a film.

I defended the film at Cannes, and I told the press that Peter was wrong. And when *Mask* got a five-minute ovation there, he looked foolish. Of course, I got my ass completely chewed out, because in Cannes they don't want you saying anything bad about the director.

In fact, I have tremendous respect for directors, the ones who nourish their actors, who give them confidence to try to be great—even if we sometimes fail in the attempt. I even have respect for Peter. You can't deny that he's made some great films.

My Baby Fat Boy . . . I love him.

Billy Sammeth

CHER'S LONG-TIME MANAGER

As part of Universal Pictures' marketing plan for the international release of *Mask,* the film was chosen by the studio as its official entry at the Cannes Film Festival. Cher was really excited about going, but she wanted to take her best friend Paulette Betts along with her. Unfortunately, there is no place in a studio's budget for "Best Friends Going to Cannes," so Cher and I concocted a story . . .

I called Anne Bennett, the head of publicity at UIP (the international arm of Universal Pictures), and explained to her that Cher needed to bring along her hair and makeup person: Paulette Betts! Hair and makeup personnel *are* an approved studio expense, so Anne readily approved Paulette. (Robert Haas was also accompanying us on the trip to Cannes. He was a health and fitness expert whose book *Eat to Win* was a bestseller at the time, and he was supervising a health and exercise regimen for Cher.)

We arrived in Cannes, and Cher needed to get her wig styled. I called Anne in her room to ask if she knew somebody who could style Cher's wig. "What about Paulette?" Anne replied. I responded like a school teacher explaining something really elementary to a student. "Oh, no, no, no . . . Paulette does Cher's *hair*. She doesn't do wigs—just *hair*."

Anne found a wig stylist who did a disastrous job, and that night Cher styled the wig herself—using my head as the wig block.

The next day Cher was in publicity hell: back-to-back interviews, press conferences, photo shoots, and paparazzi following her everywhere. Just before her tenth interview of the day, Cher told Anne that she really needed makeup. Anne frantically looked for Paulette and finally found her lunching with Robert Haas on the patio of the Hotel Martinez. She rushed up to Paulette, totally out of breath and said, "Paulette . . . Cher really needs makeup!" Paulette looked up from her salad Niçoise and dropped a plastic baggy full of Cher's cosmetics into Anne's palm. "Here it is," she said innocently.

That night an exhausted Anne Bennett came up to me (she was so proper, so English) and said, "Billy, let me ask you a question. Paulette *doesn't* do wigs, and she obviously *doesn't* do makeup . . . so what exactly *does* Paulette do?"

I spoke to Cher: "Anne has figured out that Paulette doesn't do anything that we said she did!" We had to own up to Anne that night—she was actually amused that we came up with this entire story so that Cher could bring along her best friend!

I think I've laughed more with Billy than any other person.

When the film was about to be released in Japan and Australia, I had to call Anne again. This time the conversation went something like this . . . "Remember the hairdresser that wasn't a hairdresser? Well, she can't go to Japan or Australia unless she can bring her two kids with her." By this time Anne had become a great friend of ours, so she just sighed. "Well," she said. "Cher *obviously* has to have her 'hairdresser' with her, so I guess I'll have to approve tickets for her children, too."

Me, cutting my wig on Bumper's head. (My manager Bill Sammeth's nickname.)

My First Time as a Blonde

I was forced to dye my hair red for <u>Mask</u> *because Peter* Bogdanovich said if I wore a wig it would look phony to the audience, and if the audience didn't know it was fake, he would. So the studio sent me to some schmuck, "Bernie the Discount Hair Dyer." The guy totally ruined my hair. I had black-and-red polka dots!

My hair was damaged so I kept cutting it off. Before we started filming, Renata (the woman who has made my wigs since the *Sonny and Cher Show* days) made a hairpiece that covered the back of my hair. Lori Davis had done her hair magic so the front hair was looking pretty good. But we just kept going slowly forward until it was a complete wig. No one ever knew, including Peter, that by the end of the filming my own hair was white and about two inches long.

Having blond hair was interesting, because people weren't sure exactly who I was—at least not immediately. Strangers talked to me nicer, softer than when I had black hair. When I needed directions, they'd explain them—sweetly and slowly.

I didn't feel prettier as a blonde, only lighter. For me it was a lark. I was just an honorary blonde.

My First Snub by the Golden Boy

I won best actress at Cannes for <u>Mask,</u> *and everyone* told me I would be nominated for an Academy Award—they were positive, positive, positive. Casinos in Las Vegas had me favored, so I figured a nomination was at least a possibility.

But I didn't get nominated. And the reasons people gave had nothing to do with my acting. They said I wasn't "serious" enough, or I didn't have a last name or that I dated young men and I didn't dress like "a serious actress."

I was so disappointed, and at first I wasn't going to go to the Awards. But then I thought, *What am I talking about? This is just a lot of crap. I'm going to go, but I'll go my way. (Me and Frank.) And I'm going to do it bigger and better than I've ever done it, and I did!.*

I went to Bob Mackie and said, "I have this idea. I want to look kind of like a Mohawk Indian. (Poor Chas.) And I want it to be so outrageous and so over-the-top that no one will mistake what I am doing it for."

Bob's outfit was actually beautiful, with great workmanship; it was chic in a very bizarre way. It was a homage to an Indian costume, with a black cashmere blanket and Indian symbols in black satin. There was a breastplate made in black diamonds and beads, and a giant Mohawk feather headpiece, with long earrings that went with the headdress and the breastplate. There were very low, tight pants, with a long loincloth that went to the floor. And I wore one contact—one blue eye and one brown eye.

I was living with Joshua Donen at the time, and I said to him, "Now Joshua, no matter what I look like, you're not going to be embarrassed to go with me are you?"

He said, "Sweetheart, don't worry. I'm going to be proud to take you, and it's going to be fabulous, and you're going to look beautiful."

And when it was time to go, and I came out of the bathroom with my outfit on, Joshua almost passed out. But he was so cool and adorable about it, and so brave. And then his dad, Stanley Donen, who was producing the Awards, saw me and said to Joshua, "Oh, Cher, she is the funniest thing. I just love her; this is so great." Joshua finally exhaled.

Stanley came from the golden days of Hollywood, when every star put on their finest, whether it was outrageous or demure.

When I got up on stage to present the supporting actor award, I said, "As you can see, I got my Academy handbook on how to dress as a serious actress." Everybody got hysterical. They all knew what I was talking about.

I didn't care about all the criticism that outfit got, or when David Letterman said it would have been suitable for Darth Vader's funeral. (I just hoped that it hadn't scared poor Don Ameche too much when I handed him his Oscar.) I'm not afraid to look ridiculous. It's a dirty job, but somebody's got to do it.

The First Time I Called David Letterman an Asshole

I watched David Letterman every night, and I thought he was brilliant. But sometimes I thought he went too far. When he didn't like a guest, or when he thought a guest wasn't smart enough, he would make fun of them and be just plain rude. And he was so good at it.

The *Late Night* people asked me a hundred times to come on the show, and I always said no. But then I had this huge bill—it was $26,000, or maybe $38,000—at Morgan's Hotel in New York, and so I said, "If you pay my hotel bill, I'll come on."

They said, "We can't pay that. We just pay scale." But eventually they said OK. Then Robert Morton, the show's producer, asked me, "Why haven't you come on with Dave before?"

I said, "Because I thought he was kind of an asshole."

So that night I went on, and one of the first questions David asked me was, "Tell me, Cher, why haven't you ever done my show?" He knew what I'd told Robert Morton, and he was just going to sit there and watch me squirm.

I looked at him. He looked at me. We both knew what the truth was—and that I wouldn't be able to tell the truth. And I *was* squirming. I really didn't mean to say it. I thought I was going to say something different. But then I looked at him smirking at me, and suddenly the words just jumped out of my mouth:

"Because I thought you were an asshole."

They bleeped me, but you could read my lips. My manager, Billy Sammeth, fell down on the ground. Letterman's face fell to the floor. He was laughing, but I know he was haunted by it for months. Shirley MacLaine went on the week after and said, "You know, Cher said you were an asshole, and you are."

Letterman kept going back to it. When *People* magazine asked him what was the worst thing that ever happened to him, he said, "Cher called me an asshole once on TV."

I wasn't trying to be mean-spirited; I was kind of playing with him. The truth is I liked him in spite of himself. Then he wrote me a really funny note, and we got to be kind of friends.

Not close friends, though, because he never exhales.

The First Time I Got Paid for Being a Witch

On the morning of my fortieth birthday, I woke up in New York to a call from George Miller, director of *The Witches of East-wick.* He said, "Jack Nicholson doesn't want you to play the part you want, because you're not sexy enough."

As I was talking, my kids and Paulette brought a cake up to our room in Morgan's Hotel; they had a bellman to help them carry it. They were singing happy birthday, and I was weeping in front of everybody. I felt like the girl that nobody wants to take to the prom.

Actually, it was George Miller who didn't want me for *Witches.* He'd been pressured by the studio to have me, but he kept telling me, "I don't want '*Cher*' to ruin my movie." And he used his fingers to make little quotes in the air whenever he said "Cher."

After we started rehearsal, George went into hyperspace. He'd go into this complex analysis of what the movie was really about and "the psychological depth of the character," and so on. He had a blackboard that he kept writing on, but I never had a fucking clue what he was talking about. I don't think anybody did, except maybe Jack.

Of course, once we started shooting, it was just a movie, and I had no problems with George. He excelled at filming complicated action, but talking to actors wasn't his strong suit. Now, for me that was OK. But Sue and Miche were used to working with their director and having some dialogue, and George's idea of dialogue was, "Get me a larger wind machine."

They called the three of us "the girls." As far as everyone (except Jack) was concerned, we were window dressing. They'd say, "Sue, don't take that line. Give it to Michelle, or give it to Cher—it doesn't matter."

One day Jack told them, "If you're looking for star performances from these women, you better stop treating them like extras."

We called Jack "Little Johnny," and he called us "Chair," "Soo," and "Miche." He got lunch for us every day and made us feel like we were valuable. He was just the most adorable "Little Devil" you could ever imagine.

When Jack was small, his mother and grandmother ran a beauty parlor in the back of their house, and he'd come in and sit and read his comic books and listen to the women talk. Now, he loved to come into the trailer each morning, while Sue and Miche and I were getting made up, and read his newspaper and listen to us talk. Once Kathleen Turner came out in *People* magazine with some crazy remark about how beautiful her legs were, and we were going, "I can't *believe* her." And Jack was just laughing at everything we said—I think he really cared about us.

Witches was a long shoot, and one day when I was walking off the set with what I guess was a gloomy face, Jon Peters, one of the producers and also a friend, came up to me and said, "What's the matter, Cher? You seem sad. Would you like me to buy you something? A dress? A bracelet?"

I looked at Jon and said, "What, you're Flo Ziegfeld and I'm a fucking chorus girl?"

Jon was actually trying to be nice, but the whole thing just pissed me off. I don't know if I was just being a bitch that day or was hormonally challenged. Whatever it was, Jon and I made it up at a dinner at the Ivy put together by my friend Ronni Meyer. We all laughed. I should have taken the bracelet! ⌐◦

The opening monologue of <u>The Cher Show</u>.
There's no being kind here—I sucked!

I got up during this flight from Denver to L.A. and asked my fellow passengers if anyone of them would like this baby. Chas said she would keep him if I paid for the Pampers.

Gee, Mom, Chas, and me at my mom's store, Granny's Cabbage Patch.

Ma and Da with their old noses.

My first time in the big time alone. Son came to see me here.

←

*Look at me; am I wearing a smug
look on my face or what?*

→ This shot was for a poster, but people thought it was too risqué. Boy was I ahead of my time.

I was having a real <u>Saturday Night Fever</u> moment with myself here.

I don't think I weighed a hundred pounds soaking wet in this picture.

The Hasty Pudding Award day was a blast. The boys treated me like a queen, and that doesn't suck!

→

Poor Don Ameche, he'd won his Oscar but he had to have it handed to him by the Last of the Mohicans. I don't care what anyone says, I love this outfit! Can you remember what anyone else wore to the Academy Awards this year? NO!

I loved Vincent Gardenia.
There was never a man who
was funnier or more kind.

The day we shot this
scene, I went home and
cried. I thought I was
terrible. When I saw
the movie I was shocked;
I was good!

Nicky Cage is
Ronnie Cammareri.

My fourth Golden Globe.

→ *Who could be bad working with "Little Johnny"? There's nothing but "gushie stuff" to say about this little Devil.*

What a _____ night!

I'm not sure I wasn't a fool in paradise. I only wish I could have stayed. Rob and me.

*Son and me on <u>Letterman</u>. We always
picked up like we'd never left off.*

→
*Life is good, and who
says I don't know how
to be low key?*

Elijah was my date for an Armani charity event. I was so proud to be going with my son! Isn't he handsome.

My sister has this thing about headbands and tall wiggly things.

This is my favorite picture of Chas and me.

The First Time I Got in Bed with 1,300 Snakes

Sue Sarandon was supposed to have the scene with the snakes in *Witches,* but then the director flipped them over to me. I was fine with it, as long as they weren't insects. If they'd been cockroaches, I would not have been able to do it.

The scene started with me sleeping in my bed, and these little green guys crawling in my hair. I was supposed to open my eyes and see one of them, then throw my covers off. Unfortunately, there were a couple of little snakes inside the covers, and it was like a slingshot—they got flung in the air, and one of them landed on our poor cameraman, who was completely terrified of snakes—he panicked and jumped off the crane, which was four feet off the floor.

All of a sudden, everyone's true colors started showing. It was like, "Where is everybody?" Half the crew didn't want to be there, and some of them just would not come on the stage. Leonard, my makeup man, had the prop man rig his powder puff on the end of a twenty-foot pole because he wasn't getting anywhere near me. Some friend you are, Len!

They had 1,300 snakes in that bed, and there were quite a few big ones. (The boa constrictors just wound around the lamps—they didn't really move.) The one thing I kept asking the snake wranglers was, "How would you know if there were any poison snakes in here? How does a poison snake look different from the other ones?" I didn't really like his answer, which was, "Oh, someone is supposed to go through all the snakes to make sure no poisonous ones get in here by mistake."

My only real problem was that I had this flimsy knee-length T-shirt on, and the little snakes kept getting up under it. After the first take, I said to the wranglers, "Let me pull down my T-shirt really tight, and *then* let the snakes go." Because I had to be so rough, tossing and turning after I saw the snakes in the bed, I was worried that I was going to smash the little guys, and then I'd have to act on smashed snake. Yuck! ⌒◯

My First Mook from Queens

On the eve of my fortieth birthday, I went with my friends to Heartbreak, a club where I used to go dancing in New York. I was sitting there, having a beer, and thinking, *I'm forty. I'm supposed to be old. But I feel great, like a kid.*

It was then that I saw Robert Camilletti. He had the most handsome face I'd ever seen. I looked at him like I would a beautiful statue.

I looked at Robert off and on all night, from afar, but if he looked in my direction, I turned away. At one point I got sweaty dancing, so I went off the floor to mop my face with cocktail napkins. I looked up, and Robert was just standing there, looking at me. And this time I didn't turn away.

My friend Paulette came up to talk to me, and when I didn't answer, she looked where I was looking. She grabbed my arm and said, "Come on, this is just too ridiculous." We went back to our table, and she said, "Cher, you should be ashamed of yourself." But I wasn't!

The next time I went to Heartbreak, Robert was there again. He came up to me and said, "I understand that you've been inquiring about me. If you'd ever like to call me, this is my number." He was speaking about a job. I was going to make an album after I finished all the movies I was working on, and I thought he would be great in the video.

I didn't do anything about it until three months later. One of the hairdressers on *Witches of Eastwick* was telling us this story about how she had sex with her dentist in the dentist's chair. We couldn't believe it. I said, "How could you do that?"

And she said, "It just happened."

"Well, how did it just happen?"

And she said, "It was an opportunity, and we both just took it." Michelle and I just looked at each other with our mouths open.

An opportunity. . . . I had gotten tickets for a play with Sean Penn and Madonna, but everyone was out of town for Labor Day. I had my assistant call Robert and say, "This is not a date, but Cher would like you to go with her to see a play." Then at the last minute I ran into Melanie Griffith and I asked her to come along, too. Mel was up for anything.

We met at my hotel, and when Robert came in he was very cool and confident. (Later he told me he was just a wreck, and he'd gone to the bar and had two shots before he came up.) We went to the play, and it was so weird. I was thinking, *This guy is going to hate me—he's going to think this is the dumbest date he's ever been on.*

Meanwhile, Rob was thinking, *I don't understand any of this, and I'm going to seem really stupid to her, because I don't know what's going on in this play.*

It was the last night of the play, so we went to the cast party afterwards, and then we went back to my apartment at Morgan's Hotel. We talked forever. I thought Robert was a sweet guy. But he was so young, I thought that we'd just be great friends—and I'd have this fabulous guy to hang out with whenever I came to New York.

At 3:30 in the morning, Robert jumped up to go. (He didn't say why, but he had to open this bagel bakery in Queens.) I walked him downstairs, and when I went to shake his hand, he kissed me on the cheek—just a friend kiss. I was supposed to go to Los Angeles the next day, and I told him I'd give him a call when I got back.

But the next day I just couldn't get it together to pack my bags. I had dinner with Mel that night, then we went to Heartbreak and met Robert and a friend of his named Steve. Steve was gorgeous, too. I said, "Do you come from a place where there's just handsome Italian guys? Is that what Queens is?"

When we stopped dancing at Heartbreak, we decided we wanted to go on to the China Club, but Robert said we couldn't go in their car, we'd have to take a cab. And I said, "Why can't we go in your car?"

He said, "Because there's a hole in the floorboard."

Mel and I looked at each other and started laughing, and I said,

"You think we've never been in broken-down old cars before? Let's go in your car, it'll be fine."

Robert said, "Okay, but I'm sitting over the hole."

At the China Club I started feeling uncomfortable. I didn't want to dance. And I thought, *This is ridiculous. I don't belong here with this kid. I should just go back to L.A.*

When I told Robert that I had to go pack for my flight the next morning, he asked to come back to my hotel and pick up a script I had told him I was doing after *Witches.* He was curious; it was the script for *Moonstruck.* I gave it to him, and he started to walk out, but as I went to shake his hand goodbye, he looked upset and he said, "This is not the way it's supposed to go."

I asked him to sit down. I held his hand and I could feel his pulse. It was racing. Then Robert said, "This is not the way I'd like it to go." I was confused. We just looked at each other, and it was one of those looks that became more and more and more intense. And then we kissed. We ended up talking and kissing all night long on my couch.

When we woke up the next day, we ordered orange juice and croissants, and I said, "Do you mind if I turn on the football game?"

Robert said, "You like football?"

I said yeah. His mouth fell open, and he said, "I think I love you."

It was a Giants preseason game, and after one play I said something like, "You fucking idiot, that wasn't clipping! *Jesus!* What's the matter with your eyes?"

Robert just looked at me and said, "You're the most incredible woman I've ever met."

Five days after I left New York, I called him, and we started talking. I was shooting nights, so we would talk all night long sometimes. Robert was living in his parents' house, and he'd talk to me from his basement until he had to go to the bagel shop. When I got a long weekend off from *Witches,* I flew to New York to buy an apartment, and I came there every weekend I could. Then I moved back for good and started work on *Moonstruck,* and that's when I started to fall in love with Robert.

"Mook"—
a '40s man.

He was the most well-adjusted person I'd ever met. He was just healthy and normal, like a 1940s man. His dad was the coolest guy who ever drew breath. He worked for Con Edison, and he still went with his wife to watch the sunset and hold hands. Robert's mom and his sisters were also great—they're a wonderful '40s family.

I called Robert "Mookie" after he told me that he was "just a mook from Queens." When he came into my world, it was completely foreign to him. But as young as he was, he didn't bat an eyelash. He could handle anything, and he thought that I needed him. He was always supportive of my work, which most men were intimidated by.

After I started filming *Moonstruck*, I would come home, take a shower, get into bed, and fall right asleep. Robert was working as a doorman, and he'd get in around 2:30 in the morning. Then I'd wake up. I'd plan to spend two hours with him, and we'd talk while a big smokestack blew huge puffs of smoke by our window. It was great.

When the moon got to a certain place in the sky, I'd know we'd gone past our two-hour limit. And I'd say, "Robert, goddamn it, I have to go back to sleep—look where the moon is!" It seems so strange that the moon played such a big part in my real life while I was shooting *Moonstruck.*

Robert was only twenty-two when I met him, and I guess you could say we had nothing in common. He was little when Sonny and I were on TV. He hadn't read the books I'd read, or been the places I'd been, and he didn't know the old movies I loved, and we didn't agree that much on music. There really weren't many things we shared in common.

But those things didn't seem to be that important when we were together. Whenever I had a day off, we loved to go to two or three movies in a row—"movie marathons," we called them—or go dancing. Or just walking around in the Village, where we found a strange little café that had fabulous macaroni and cheese and homemade pecan pie. Or we'd stay home and play gin or double solitaire. We just loved being together.

We didn't have exactly the same sense of humor, but Robert was a great laugher—he had a big-man laugh from his stomach, and he was very ready to use it. He was a great audience, and I loved making him laugh. I had more fun with Robert than I would ever have dared to imagine.

But, most of all, we'd talk. No one can understand what it feels like when your whole life has been One Big Criticism. And then one day, a wonderful man says, "Sure, you're not perfect, but it wasn't perfection I was searching for." Robert was hoping for a woman who was trying to be as good a person as she could possibly be—and he wanted to feel needed, to take care of her. He was definitely the grown-up in our relationship. He was a true man in every sense of the word.

The hardest thing for me to understand was that he simply seemed to love me as I was. We are best friends to this day, and I will never not love him. ～◯

The First Time I Fought to Choose My Costar

Nicolas Cage got very mixed reviews for <u>Peggy Sue</u> Got Married—a lot of people thought his performance was too weird. But I loved Nicky in that movie. I thought that anybody who had the guts to expose his ass like that was the right person to play Ronnie Cammareri in *Moonstruck.* Nicky would be prepared to go all the way. The first time I read the line, "Give me the big knife, I want the big knife," I could only hear him saying it.

But the studio didn't want him; they wanted Peter Gallagher. Now, I think that Peter is a great actor, but in my mind, he wasn't nuts. Nicky was *nuts,* and "nuts" is what we needed.

I did a screen test with Nicky, and then I did one with Peter, and of course they still wanted Peter. But I had Nicky in my brain, and I could not think of doing the movie without him.

So I went against the studio and told them I wouldn't do the film without Nicky. I was right—he *was* Ronnie Cammareri.

Norman was a brilliant, insightful director. He literally talked me through the scene when Nicky and I are at the Met watching <u>La Bohème</u>. We were looking at an empty stage, listening to the music, while Norman told us the story. He told it so well, I cried.

The First Time "I Got You Babe" Made People Cry

In February of 1988, Sonny and I went on David Letterman together.

I was in my dressing room, getting ready to go on, when Chas came in and said, "Mom, I think they're going to ask you to sing with Dad." I said, "Chas, that's crazy. We haven't rehearsed anything—how would the band even know what key your dad and I sing in?" But I couldn't think about it, because I was worried about "I Found Someone," the song I was about to do. (I had asked Son to be in the control room when I rehearsed the song earlier that day, because I needed him to tell me if I was doing it right. I hadn't done an album for five years.)

When I finished singing my song, I sat down on the couch between David and Son. David and I got into it a little bit—he did his number on my outfit and my tattoos, and I mouthed the word "asshole," just for old time's sake. Then Son and I started joking back and forth; there was a very Sonny-and-Cher kidding-around kind of feeling in the room. It was like Son and I had never split up; we didn't miss a beat. Then David did what Chas warned me he would do. He said to me, "Is there any chance that you two would sing for us?"

The crowd started cheering and whistling. Son said he'd do it, so I said I'd try. We hadn't been onstage together for years. But the normal rules never applied to us, and as soon as I started, "They say we're young and we don't know . . . ," it was like no time had passed at all. We just hit our stride immediately. It was great, at least at the beginning. It was like sharing a private joke with someone you'd known forever. And it felt really good that we hadn't lost that thing that we had, the thing that I had never had with anyone else.

But then the whole vibe of the room changed dramatically. It was like I was on a horse, galloping along in one direction, and then suddenly the horse made a right turn without me. It was the strangest feeling I'd ever felt in an audience. Chas was in the booth; she was crying, and so was Sonny's wife Mary. So were some of the *Late Night* pages. I could see people in the audience out of the corner of my eye, and some of them were crying, too.

I started to feel guilty, responsible. I just thought, *Oh, God.* I glanced over at Son, and in that split second I saw that he was rubbing his eyes. And I thought, *I've got to hold myself together—I don't want to do this publicly.* These were our own private, complicated feelings, and I didn't want to share them on TV. I didn't want to cry about us on TV.

I knew that I had to be the strong one for Son for the first time in my life. I held myself together. And we finished "I Got You Babe." ∼◦

Son and me on Letterman. There really are no words to truly describe the moment for me. All I can say is for the first time in our lives, I felt like the parent—like I needed to protect him.

My First (Golden) Dream Man

On the day of the 1988 Academy Awards, Sonny called me and said, "I know you're going to win tonight. Don't worry about it—it's a cinch." And he said, "You'd better hope I win tomorrow"—he was about to be elected mayor of Palm Springs. "If I don't win, I'm going to have to leave the country." I told him that I knew he would win and I meant it. I wasn't so positive about myself. The night of the Oscars there was a huge traffic jam even before we got to the front of the Shrine Auditorium. At one point we had to jump out of our car and start running, because the first presentation was for best supporting actress, Olympia Dukakis's category. I wanted to be there for it. I felt great when she won. Then I went up with Nicky Cage to present the best supporting actor award, and when the winner turned out to be Sean Connery, I started laughing. The week before I'd given him a BAFTA (English Oscar), so in the space of two weeks I'd given him both of the Academy Awards he won in his life. I guess I was lucky for him.

I didn't feel like an alien anymore—after doing three films in a year, I figured I was pretty much here to stay. I even thought that it wouldn't be so horrible if I lost this time.

That year, for some unknown reason, they'd moved my category close to last. *Why did they have to move it this year?* I wanted to get it over with. I was trying to concentrate on everything, divert my mind as much as possible.

When Paul Newman came out and started to read the nominees, I lost my hearing. I felt like I was in an altered state, like being underwater; I heard the noise, but I really wasn't *hearing* properly. I was picturing myself in one of those little boxes on TV, trying to be all smiley faced and calm as I could be, but I lost all sense of reality.

Then Paul took a deep breath, and I thought, *That's it. I lost. It's not me. You don't need a big breath to say "Cher."* So I relaxed, and then he said, "Cher, for *Moonstruck.*" Robert jumped up, and my entire row jumped up, and what I didn't realize until I watched a videotape later was that everybody in the whole place stood up and applauded.

A million things were running through my mind at five hundred miles an hour. I kissed Robert, I grabbed my kids. I turned around, I took about five steps, tripped on my shawl, and lost an earring. And I said, "Shit!" and I wondered if a camera was on my face when I said it.

As I walked up to the stage, electricity was streaming out of my eyeballs—*Where am I? What is this? Who are all these people?* I had practiced my acceptance speech for my whole life in the shower, but I didn't have anything prepared that night. I was going to say something, and then I just kind of collapsed on the podium and started laughing, and nothing came out exactly right.

I couldn't really see anybody from the stage, and I hadn't made a list. I totally forgot to thank Norman Jewison, or Nicky Cage or anybody else in the cast. I didn't even thank the Academy. Afterward everyone was pissed because I thanked my hairdresser and my makeup man, but the truth was, we had just made three movies together back to back with *no* days off, and the two of them were my only constant companions through all three. And I was in shock. I did thank Meryl Streep for teaching me so much about acting, and I did remember how my mother always wanted me to be something.

Then I went backstage to talk to all the rooms of press people. I was thinking, *You have to remember this night forever,* not realizing that I would never be able to forget it. I don't remember one question from the interviews, but I can still get the feeling I had that night every time I think about it. I felt lifted off my feet, just floating from room to room and never touching the ground.

I floated past Audrey Hepburn, my hero, and she grabbed my hand and said, "I'm so glad you won—I wanted you to win." And that was almost as good as getting the award.

Then I posed with Michael Douglas, who'd won best actor for *Wall Street,* but my feet were killing me, so I took my shoes off and I posed,

How can I tell you the excitement I was feeling?
"I'm on top of the world, Ma." And still when I
look at my Oscar, I smile.

standing on my tiptoes. They kept trying to take the Oscar away from me (yeah, fat chance), to have my name put on it, but they weren't getting it out of my hands that night. I held it tightly in my hand the whole time, and it's really heavy, but it felt like a feather to me. It was a permanent fixture, like my hand had grown into it.

Then the Awards were over, and we went home. I skipped the parties; I'm not really that big of a party girl. We had a pizza party on my bed—pepperoni and half cheese for me. My mom was there, and my kids and my sister, and Robert, and my assistant Deb. We put the Oscar up on the mantelpiece, and everyone was saying, "Ooohh, can I touch it? Can I hold it?"

It's hard for me to explain how great I felt. I know you're not supposed to act too excited about these things. But what can I say? I'm not that cool! It was one of the great nights of my life.

Now I have a second chance to tell my friends how much they meant to me, and how they helped make my performance what it was.

Norman, you are one of the three great directors I've worked with. Without you, I would only have been half as good.

Nicky, you will always be Ronnie to me.

Olympia—who could ever want a better friend and actress for a mother? (Even if Norman did make you change your hair color.)

Vincent, I love you as much as anyone I've ever known and wherever you are, I hope you know this.

Feodor Chaliapin—*Ciao, bello, bello amore mio.*

Julie Bovasso, without your help to find my accent, I would have been only a shadow of Loretta. And no one else could ever have said, "It's Johnny Camma-*re*-ri" the way you did.

Louis Guss, you were the sweetest, most up person on the set! Thank you, Louie.

Danny Aiello, you were so much fun for me—and so kind, even when I almost killed you in the tunnel.

And finally you, Patrick Palmer. You have my love and respect forever.

I was simply lucky—God must have been smiling down on me—when you all came into my life.

The First Time I Had to Make Bail for Someone

From the beginning of our relationship, I told Robert, "We have to enjoy these days while we have them, because if any one of the movies or the album I'm doing becomes successful, our whole life will change."

But even I didn't expect what happened after I won the Academy Award!

The press coverage became insane, it was more invasive than I'd ever remembered. The tabloids were bigger and meaner than they'd ever been. Everyone was hoping you had some horrible secret you were hiding, and with all the paparazzi selling their pictures to the highest bidder, there was no place you were safe. Even inside your own house.

What made the media more carnivorous, in my opinion, was the age difference between Robert and me. An older man with a younger woman is just life, but an older woman with a younger man is a story. For no apparent reason, people started attacking Robert unmercifully. Howard Stern made it his life's work to trash me and everyone in my family. He'd fillet Robert every chance he could, but Robert was great about it. That's the difference between them—one's a man, the other is only a male.

I also had crazy people coming at me from everywhere. Two guys crawled over my fence one night. Then there was a bizarre guy who'd walk up to my gate and ring the bell incessantly, night after night, and another one who actually kicked in my front door. (He was taken away, and then he started calling me from jail.) And there was a guy with a shaved head who came all the way from San Francisco to pitch a tent on my lawn and tell me that he'd quit smoking.

Robert and I still thought we could manage to live in our fishbowl. But then some aspiring press agent planted the rumor that Robert and I were about to get married and have a huge wedding. It wasn't true, but it stirred the paparazzi into a frenzy. They hit my home in Benedict Canyon, heavy and hard. They camped out front for a week at a time and went through our garbage; there was no rest from these people.

My home had a really long driveway, and the cops would tell these guys that it was private property. But when the cops weren't around, the paparazzi would jump back on the driveway, and they'd chase us whenever we left the house.

One day we tried to go someplace, and a car came up alongside of us, and another one drove behind us, trying to get a better picture. It was a scary experience; they almost drove us off the road into a ditch. The next day I had a doctor's appointment, and Robert came up with an idea: He'd go out in my car first, be a decoy, and then I could go out in another car.

I thought the plan worked well, and I got back from the doctor without being noticed. Robert came back a little later. He went to make a left into my driveway, and these two paparazzi jumped out in front of him. When he swerved so he wouldn't hit them, he crashed our car.

Robert wasn't hurt, but he was so upset about crashing the car that he wanted to rip those guys apart. He started to run after them, and then he saw their Toyota and went inside it and ripped out the phone instead. Then he came up to the house, huffing and puffing, and told me what happened.

When the police came, they told the paparazzi, "It's just an accident—work it out with your insurance company." But these guys claimed that Robert had tried to kill them, and they'd barely escaped by running away. It was a ridiculous story, because they were the most out-of-shape, overweight photographers I'd ever seen (and I've seen some pretty awful photographers in my life). If Robert had wanted to kill them, he would have caught them in a heartbeat.

Then the police said they'd have to arrest Robert, even though they didn't want to, and take him in. I started screaming at them, "You're going to do *what?* What in the fuck is the matter with you guys? Are you insane?" You know he didn't try to kill those scum-sucking pigs. (Perhaps I've gone too far? Nah!)

Robert was charged with assault with a deadly weapon. I followed him down to the Beverly Hills police station to make bail. I was sitting by myself on a bench inside the station, waiting for him to be released, when all of a sudden there were about a hundred and fifty press people, including camera crews. They were all shouting questions at me; it was like something out of a Fellini movie. I had no idea that the press was allowed to come inside a police station. I felt like a caged animal.

I just became numb. I didn't hear anybody, I didn't see anything. I paid Robert's bail, and my friend picked him up at the back of the jail. I got up and went straight to the car; the press followed us. Robert was humiliated.

The paparazzi got more than $150,000 for their pictures of Robert, and of me screaming at the cops. Robert got a fine and an unbelievable amount of community service. (People have committed murder in this country and gotten off lighter than Robert did in court.) He'd been humiliated in jail, just treated like shit. Some cop looked in his cell and said, "Oh, yeah, you're the wop that's fucking Cher!" It was the final straw for him. He said to me, "I can't bear to be under this microscope all the time. I love you, but I need to go back home—I miss my life." He left Los Angeles and went back to New York.

The First Time I Assisted at Surgery

After I did the movie Mask, *I was lucky enough to become* involved with a charity called Children's Craniofacial Association. They needed someone to raise money and awareness for them, and I seemed to be the right person for the job.

I went to Washington, DC, to meet everyone and go to an event. That's when I met the kids. They were unbelievable—so lively, so bright, so *beautiful.* Yes, their little faces were misshapen, but their little life forces were strong and brilliant! It was literally love at first sight for all of us. I'm not trying to be corny; that's just exactly what happened.

That night, all the kids and their parents came back to eat burgers in my suite. After the kids fell asleep, the parents started to tell me about the hell that their children had to endure. The endless, painful operations—as many as thirty or forty! These children would be willing to go through so much for such small victories.

I have always been so concerned with the way I look. And then for me to be around these little kids who would give anything just to have their eyes and nose in the right places—it made me feel ashamed. It rocks you to your foundation; it makes you think about what beauty really is.

In every city I went to on tour, the local Craniofacial chapter would bring kids backstage to hang with me before the show. We did this all over the world, and I was in complete shock when I saw the kids outside America. Over here, a child would be in the middle of their scores of operations. There was always a succession of surgeries, starting when the child was as young as a year old, to keep up with bone development. But in Europe and other places in the world, I'd see grown-up people who'd never had anything done at all. It was alarming.

In Australia I met a girl named Marie Jatejic, who had neurofibromatosis. She was thirteen years old, and was such a precious little girl. I was back home a few months later, and one day I just decided to call Marie and her mom to see what we could do.

We got Marie's pictures sent over to Medical City Dallas Hospital, one of the very best hospitals in the United States for craniofacial work, and they scheduled the surgery. *People* magazine wanted to do a story about Marie, which was great—not only would it help her, but it would make people aware of the devastating problem.

The smell of a hospital always made me sick, and I'm deathly afraid of operating rooms, but for some reason I decided I wanted to be there with Marie. When they started the surgery, I was on the opposite side of the room. Then I moved a little closer, and I thought, *I'm okay.* Then a little closer, and I thought, *This is really interesting.* It wasn't like an amputation—it was something that I knew would make Marie happy because she'd look substantially better and therefore she'd feel so much better about herself.

I got closer and closer until I was right at Marie's armpit—they had her arm out so that the anesthesiologist could read her vitals. The surgeon, Dr. Monroe, was around the other way, looking toward Marie's face from over her shoulder. At the end of the surgery, I started telling him that I thought he wasn't doing it right: "Don't you think you could just take a little bit more out, because she's a girl, you know . . ."

And the doctor said, "No, this is enough for now, Cher. As the tumor grows, we'll watch it and we'll go in again later, but this is all we can take out for right now."

And I said, "But don't you want to do something with her nose?"

"No, that's the soft-tissue work. We'll do it later."

The surgery lasted eight hours. They needed two or three different teams, but Dr. Monroe never left. I went out just to go to the bathroom and give updates to Marie's mom. I also massaged Marie's hands, because even when people are unconscious, they respond to sound and touch.

There are just a few truly heightened experiences in your life, things that take you into a space that's new and exhilarating. It was that way when I had my children and when I won the Oscar. And it was that way when I watched Marie's operation. ⁓

Note: If you have a child with a facial disfigurement, whether the result of birth defect, disease or trauma, it is vital to get help early, and *only* from a qualified craniofacial specialist. Children with facial disfigurements have a difficult road ahead of them, and it is essential that they receive the proper medical care. Consulting a plastic surgeon who is *not* a specialist trained in the surgical management of problems involving the face and head can result in disastrous complications. Don't make this painful mistake.

Please—if you have a child with a facial disfigurement, I urge you to contact the Children's Craniofacial Association. It is their mission to improve the quality of life for facially disfigured individuals and their families. *They can help.*

Children's Craniofacial Association
P.O. Box 280297
Dallas, TX 75228

Tel: 1-800-535-3643

Contact: Charlene Smith

My First Infomercial
—or—
How to Destroy Your Life in One Easy Lesson

By the time I made <u>Mermaids</u>, in 1990, my immune system was completely shot. My glands were always swollen, and I was on and off antibiotics for two years straight. It was a horrendous cycle. I was sick and depressed and couldn't work.

Around this same time my friend Lori Davis asked me to be the spokesperson for her hair products. I used her products anyway and knew they were great. Also, I thought maybe this would be a way to make money while I was too sick to work. So even though it wasn't my life's dream to do an infomercial, I said yes. But my agent, Ronnie Meyer, said "Don't do it. Don't do it. Don't do it." I wanted him to be wrong because I was just out of gas. But I told him I would talk to Lori and tell her I couldn't do it. I was going to tell Lori, but when I walked into her salon, she came up to me and gave me this huge hug. "You know what I just realized?" she said. "I couldn't do this without you. I'm so terrified to be in front of a camera." So between her tears and my being just plain whipped, I did the infomercial. It didn't occur to me that I'd be on every channel, twenty-four fucking hours a day, seven days a week. By the time I realized how smarmy I looked, it was too late. *Letterman* and *Saturday Night Live* started doing parodies of me.

The backlash was huge. I was riding so high after the Academy Award. Now I was a joke. There's nothing like an infomercial to slam-dunk your ass. I stopped getting movie offers. My agent said, "I can't get you a job! Nobody wants to know about you." It was like that scene in *Tootsie* when Sydney Pollack tells Dustin Hoffman that not only could he not get him a job in New York, he couldn't get him a job anywhere! I had sold my credibility. I had *really* fucked up! The worst thing about it was I had no one to blame but myself! (God, I hate it when that happens.) Why couldn't I have thought to sell something meaningful, like . . . Planet Hollywood. ⌒◟

The First Time I Learned My Daughter Was Gay

When I found out that Chas was gay, I went ballistic!
What added insult to injury was finding out that everyone else in the solar system knew but me! My assistant, my sister, the gardener, etc. I was angry, I was hurt, I felt so left out.

I called Chas in New York. That's when I found out that her dad knew. I screamed and yelled at Chas, and then I hung up. We didn't talk for almost a week.

I was out of my mind. I had a very un-Cher-like reaction when I found out. But when something hits you, you react—you don't stop and think about it.

Once I calmed down, and I thought about it, I asked Chas to come to L.A. with her girlfriend, Heidi. After they were there for a couple of days, it didn't seem so hard to accept. Her girlfriend was funny. Chas was happy and she looked beautiful.

In the back of my mind, I'd always known. I just hoped it wasn't true. I always hoped it was a phase—that Chas was a tomboy like I had been and she'd grow out of it.

I had to figure out what I was most upset about. It wasn't just that I was the last person to know.

You never know what you believe until you're confronted with it. I've had gay friends my whole life.

But I didn't want my daughter to be gay.

On one level, I think I accepted it immediately. But it took me time to go through all the different steps to truly *accept* it. And there's no jumping over any steps. You have to allow yourself the time to really change.

I had so much guilt for a while. I thought it must have been something I did wrong. If I hadn't been away so much, working all the time, if I'd stayed home and baked more cookies, all the crap that single parents are haunted by. When my kids were growing up, I always felt like I was juggling eight balls in the air at one time, trying to be all things to all people at once! And failing miserably.

As a parent, your job is to try and fix things. But then you have to realize that you can't control who your children are, or what they want to do with their lives.

I had to realize that Chas had to live her life in the way that made her happy; she was still Chas. She was still the same person.

She was my child, and it wasn't good enough for me to *just* accept her. I had to support her and be proud of *who she was.* ⟞⟝

Chastity Bono

CHER'S DAUGHTER

When I was growing up, clothes were always a struggle between me and my mother. My taste has always been much more conservative than hers. If I dressed in a masculine, preppy way—like wearing Lacoste shirts before they became a unisex fashion thing—it seemed to bother her. But if I dressed masculine in a rebel or hip style, she could relate to it.

I remember a particular Halloween in the sixth grade where I went as a Hell's Angel—to be honest, I'm not sure whether it was my idea or hers. When I was younger, we'd get fancy Halloween costumes from Bob Mackie's place. (It made my mother nervous, because I always wanted to dress up as a male character, like Dracula or Wolfman.)

But the Hell's Angel costume was neat, because my mother totally threw herself into it—she did everything. I ended up wearing her leather vest and a T-shirt, and her motorcycle boots, and a leather hat. And she painted a tattoo on my arm and a scar on my face, and she wound up coming to this Halloween fair at our school. I remember how cool and special it made me feel for her to help me get that together.

That was the last Halloween I dressed up, and it was one time that my clothes weren't an issue. My mother was able to put our differences aside and do something for me that made me feel good.

*All I can think when I
look at these pictures is,
Isn't she adorable. I'm so
lucky she's my daughter.*

My son is extremely intelligent and talented. He has a very sensitive nature, which he tries to keep hidden. I love him.

Born to play—
Elijah.

My First Big Lesson on Foreign Policy

I campaigned for Jimmy Carter in 1980, and I had dinner with him the first night he ate in the White House. I remember how he talked about helping the country's economy by actually *helping* the people—by giving them jobs and incentives. He had all these plans and was so excited about them. But he was unable to accomplish all these things because he was too honest. Jimmy Carter didn't care about serving the rich at the expense of everyone else.

I had no expectations or illusions about the Government (not to be confused with "our *system* of government," which I know is the best in the world), but I still wasn't prepared for what I saw when I went to a screening of *Panama Deception*. I just sat there, stunned. The whole audience was stunned. We'd been told that our invasion of Panama was a bloodless coup—that we were in and out—but that's not what happened at all.

The people who put on the screening of *Panama Deception* said that they didn't have enough money to pay for their negative costs. So I gave them what it cost for the negative. I believe we need *all* the information! I've heard what we say and I've seen what we do. I thought the worst thing about Panama was how nobody was reporting what really happened. Where was the real news? Why weren't we getting the truth?

People had this idea that George Bush was some kind of bumbling, smiling nice guy. But George Bush was the head of the C.I. fucking A.! He was the Anti-Christ.

I have no faith in a government that doesn't take care of its veterans. We let them risk their lives and then we treat them like shit. And our old people! We should be truly ashamed of the conditions that we force the people of the older generation to live under. Some dogs live better than our old people. And what about those children who go to bed hungry in the richest country in the world. Or the people who don't have medical care. (Oh, let's talk about HMO's, what a fucking joke.) Or the rotten schools! The whole system is run for the profit of Big Business. The people get the leftovers, the scraps! And then they try and keep the people pacified by giving them Sega and McDonald's and television and drugs. Bullshit.

Please, can we talk? (Is that too Joan Rivers of me?) If Congress would only stop wasting our time and money chasing a president who can govern his country better than his dick—and a rotund little intern whose quest in life seems to be perfecting the art of the blow job and who thinks a semen-stained dress makes a lovely family heirloom . . . (C'mon Monica, didn't anyone ever tell you that cleanliness is next to godliness???) Okay, I can't stop now you've got me started—I have all these pent-up emotions!

Let's talk about this whole bullshit affair. First of all, just how fucking far does this idiot McCarthy—sorry, I mean Starr—get to? Also, as I recall, the really BIG scandals have always happened while the Republicans were in office. Teapot Dome, Watergate, Iran-contra . . . C'mon! If you just do the math alone, you'd realize we owe the Democrats a couple from the free-throw line. It also seems to be that the Republicans don't care what laws they break when it comes to keeping the White House Democrat-free. Nixon broke every law on the books to keep McGovern from getting in, and now this entire Congress is willing to break laws to get Clinton out. C'mon, you guys. You reek of desperation!

And speaking of reeking, I think every person in Congress should be made to testify about their sex lives in front of a Grand Jury—then we'd get some real answers to the question of the hour. If you have the choice to lie to either your spouse or the Grand Jury about your extramarital affairs, which one is less scary? Oh, I could go on and on. But so could you, right? Sorry.

Maybe I'm cynical. I'm a disappointed idealist. And there's *no one* angrier than that. I used to think that the Republicans were the bad guys and the Democrats were the good guys. I'm not sure anymore. Maybe the Democrats just dress better and have a better sense of humor. Then again, maybe not.

My First Visit to Armenia

In 1993, some people approached me about going to Armenia. They wanted to shed light on how desperate the situation was over there, and they thought I could help.

The Armenians were still recovering from the '88 earthquake, and now they were at war with the Azerbaijanis. They had no money and no natural resources, and the Soviets had let everything decay. So they were just stuck up in the mountains with nothing.

I agreed to go. We boarded an old 707 cargo plane out of Heathrow, the kind they'd been using for thirty years. Our seats were bolted in to the back section of the tail. Taking off was next to impossible because the plane was so loaded down. We carried a huge amount of supplies: medicine, clothing, toys, powdered food for the Armenians, plus fresh food for our group, because there was virtually no food where we were going.

The flight was so rough that we all had to hold our own canisters of oxygen in our laps, in case anything happened. I just knew we were going to get killed on that plane, I was sure of it. *I must be nuts, I must be nuts, we're all going to get killed,* I kept saying to myself. (I'm such an optimist.)

Armenia is a difficult place to land in, because it's circled by high mountains, and you've got to come over them and then dip right down. There's no margin for error. There are no lights, so you have to get there before it gets dark. We just barely touched down in time; it got dark as we hit the runway.

Somehow I knew when we landed that this trip would be different than any other I'd ever taken.

We stayed in what was once a beautiful old hotel. But now there was no electricity, so we had to carry our bags up five flights, with only a flashlight to light our way. And there was no running water, except for two hours a day (and you never knew which two hours it would be—it was different every day), and no heat. Each guest was allowed one blanket and one candle. We'd all sit around our candles at night and tell stories, and laugh and laugh. (We laughed a lot. You'd think that wouldn't have been the case but it was.) I slept with all my clothes on all the time, even my boots, because I was freezing.

The people of Yerevan were gracious and kind. They were so unselfish. When we went to someone's home, they would offer us tea and cakes. We knew it was probably their whole week's allotment of food, and yet they wanted to share what they had with us.

People would be walking arm in arm in the main square, in their finest clothes, even if they had patches all over them. Or they'd sit in these beautiful old coffee shops—just sitting and talking, because there was no coffee.

It was amazing to see that every tree in sight had been cut down for firewood. People were slaughtering lambs and making shishkebab right there on the city streets. They kept warm by standing next to fires lit in garbage cans. But no one acted desperate. Nobody begged, and the poorest people still grew flowers in their yards. People were still making an effort. They were hardy and smart, and struggling against unbelievable odds.

And it was the only place I'd ever been where everyone looked like me.

I was everywhere; I went fifty places in a day and I was everywhere. I went to the University of Yerevan, where the kids were hungry to learn everything they could about America. It was a place they only knew about from books and movies. They asked me a thousand questions—about everything from cowboys to Jack Nicholson and what young people did and wore in America. They were just like kids anywhere, but Armenia is a hard place to be young.

It's a hard place to be at any age.

I went to one of the many orphanages there. This was a heart-wrenching experience for me, because all these children's parents had been killed in the fighting, and they had no prospects of being adopted and they were so adorable. We'd brought toys, and I gave the children stuffed animals and trucks, games and even my old nemesis, Barbie! The little girls loved the Barbie dolls. (I've always hated that blond bimbo, but that day I made a temporary truce.)

I am not a person who is used to roughing it, but somehow none of the hardships mattered. When you meet people living ten to a room, and they've lost everything they have, including their sons and daughters in the war, and they come up to you, crying, to kiss your hand—it throws a whole new light on your superficial life.

One of my nicest, most memorable days was spent at Etchmiazin Church. I met a stone-cutter there, and don't ask me why, but I'd wanted to cut stone all my life. This man let me sit by his side, and he taught me to do it with him. I could have stayed there with him forever.

It's amazing how you stop taking basic things for granted. One night the lights went on, and we all started clapping. One time I had a chance to take a bath in three inches of lukewarm water, and it was a luxury just to sit in it for a minute, which was how long it took the water to become ice cold.

Armenia was the strangest trip I've ever taken, and the most difficult one. But it was also the most rewarding one—a trip I will remember as long as I live.

Armenia was one of my most bittersweet experiences. These people had to cut down the last trees in their parks and break up the furniture in their homes for firewood to keep these orphaned children and themselves warm. We brought toys, medical supplies and other necessities on a cargo plane from England, but it was a drop in the ocean.

Me and the big men in Armenian politics. I actually tried to get out of this meeting, but it was important that I play the game.

My First Time I Tried to Catch a Man with a Golden Ring

It started as a work situation. (Oh, it's so cliché.)

It was nothing.

He wasn't great looking. He wasn't the most artistic person I've ever known, for sure. There was nothing about him that was obviously special.

He was married, no kids, and it seemed like a very strange situation. He kept telling me what a great marriage he had, but then he'd say that he couldn't talk to his wife about his work. She was consumed by her job, and they didn't spend any time together. And I finally said, "If it's so wonderful, how come you're not talking to her about your dreams? Which part of your life with her is the wonderful part?"

We were very connected, but he felt guilty and torn. He said, "I'm a coward. And if I left my wife, how do I know you'd still be there?"

We were living in different locations, but it wasn't over between us. Then, for some unknown reason, his wife called me and said, "This is an uncomfortable situation [no shit], and I'm not sure what I expect to get out of this conversation."

I said, "All right, then let's just take a stab at it."

She said, "First of all, what do you see in my husband?"

I said, "If you don't know what I see in him, I can't explain it to you."

And then she said, "But you're *Cher*. What do you want with *him?*"

I thought it was such an amazing thing for a wife to say about her husband. Maybe she had the idea that fame makes you different from other people when it comes to love, or maybe she just didn't think very much of her husband.

She asked me what I expected to happen, and I said, "Well, if I'm lucky, he'll leave you and be with me. And if I'm unlucky, he'll stay with you." (Now I'm not sure which of us was the lucky one.)

She'd initiated the conversation, but I don't think she had quite prepared herself for my response. We kept talking, and it was the strangest conversation. We talked calmly, even cordially. There was never a hint of anger from her. At one point I said to her, "Doesn't it bother you that he wears a ring that I gave him?"

She said, "Well, it's a really lovely ring." Her answer was so difficult for me to understand. If I had been her, I would've cut his fucking finger off. ⟶

My First Time as a Director

Demi Moore's production company was doing a trilogy about abortion called *If These Walls Could Talk* for HBO, and they offered me a part in one of the segments. I said that I'd act in it if I could direct the segment. I wanted to direct. (But everybody wants to direct. So what else is new?) I was truly hoping that I would be good at it, because everyone knows that actresses have the life expectancy of a fruit fly.

The first problem was that the script just wasn't right. Annie Heche and Jada Pinkett said, "We want to work with you, but we don't like the script." And I said, "You don't have to trust me as a director, but please trust me as an actor. I won't make you say anything you don't believe."

The studio got worried when I told them I was rewriting the script. I don't blame them; how did I get the idea that I could do *that?* And where was I going with it? So we hired a good writer to get a couple of the scenes into shape. Then I went over it, and I changed what I thought needed changing. I gave the studio what I did as I did it, and they got more comfortable with me as time went by.

The first day I walked on the set, I was pretty petrified, but I thought, *Well, I'm here, I might as well just do it.* And soon I was thinking, *This is so much fun!* It was definitely a lot of work, and it really tested my stamina. But I loved it from the beginning.

I had new respect for all the good directors I've worked with, because the director sets the entire atmosphere of the picture. You wear all kinds of hats, and you've got to be accessible always to everyone. You go from one person asking you a question to the next person asking you questions, all day long. The set designer comes to you and says, "How does this room look to you?" Or the cameraman says to you, "What about this angle?" Or the costume designer comes to you and says, "Come down and look at this actor's wardrobe and tell us what you think." And then you have to look at the wardrobe and consult with the actress, because clothes are really a sort of shorthand to the characters for some actors. (Me included.)

When someone asked me something and I wasn't sure of my opinion, I sounded them out first and got as much information as I could. But then I had to give them a real answer, even if I wasn't sure, and I just followed my instincts. I might be wrong, but *someone* had to decide.

I made fifty decisions a day when we were doing *If These Walls Could Talk.* It was fun keeping all those plates in the air, but it was also relentless. I remember sitting there one day and thinking, *No one's looking at me. If I ran to the toilet now, I could actually get there.*

When we were done shooting for the day, I had to watch the dailies, to make sure I had everything I needed. Then I went home dead and exhausted. It was stressful for me, because that's when I worried that I hadn't made the right choices. Or that I wouldn't make the right decisions the next day, because there were so many people counting on me, and I had to be in top form.

I loved my actors so much. I also found that I had to be different with each person—you have to know how to listen to them and know how they need you to talk to them so you can give them the help they need. Diana Scarwid had played my girlfriend in *Silkwood,* and she's a very tender person, so I had to talk with her more softly. But Annie and Jada and I had a down-the-middle, no-bullshit way of working together. We laughed a lot, but we were all no-nonsense girls.

I had had an abortion right before I got pregnant with my son Elijah. I felt that was important for my directing, because, in my mind, experience is always better than pretending. There was one thing I told Annie Heche, and she got it so perfectly. I said, "Annie, when I was lying on the table, I didn't make any sound. I didn't sob; I didn't do anything. But the tears were just draining out of my eyes." You don't really know what it's going to be, and then you hear the sound of the suction machine, and *you* die a little, too.

I used things from all the great directors I'd worked with. For instance, the last thing I'd tell an actor before we shot a scene: "I don't care if you follow the script exactly. You know what we have to get across here." Once you get that out of the way, it makes an actor more comfortable actually saying the words that are in the script—it's no longer confining. Artists need freedom, even when they don't choose to use it.

That was from Robert Altman.

I learned from Mike Nichols that you don't have to tell someone what to do. You can tell them a story instead, engage them. And by the end of the story, they'll know what to do.

And I learned from Norman Jewison about giving people a lot of feedback, right there on the spot. When we did *Moonstruck,* Norman was the first director I ever had who would laugh during a scene, and it startled me at first, but then when I got used to it it was a great thing for me. So every time we did a scene that went well in *If These Walls Could Talk,* I would show the actor how excited I was with the work. And in truth, I *was* excited. I love to be entertained; I love good work.

I was glad that I had a tiny role as the doctor, so it didn't get in the way of my work as director. I didn't worry about myself. I was so not into myself.

After nine days of shooting, I started looking at the assemblage, which is where you put all the pieces together, in order, and then you go in and rip them apart again. My editor, Peter Honess (who was nominated for an Oscar for his work on *L.A. Confidential*), would tell you that I was very scrupulous about this. I took such a long time and went over every second of film; I wanted to get my actors' best, best, best performances. I was doing all kinds of tricks, like slipping dialogue from one take to another. I got everybody's best performance by sticking pieces of film together from different takes.

Editing takes patience and concentration, and I loved doing it.

I made what I thought was the best assemblage, and then people from the production company asked to look at it. And all of a sudden,

I became this *auteur,* and I didn't mind if they looked at it, but I wasn't sure I wanted anyone telling me what to do with *my* picture. (Who was I, Orson Welles?) But after I looked at their notes and started to try some of their suggestions, I found things that none of us had thought about. It made me realize that I must be open to ideas from people I respect, ideas other than my own, for the good of the project.

If These Walls Could Talk got the highest ratings ever for an original HBO movie. It was so exciting for me—there was an unbelievable amount of satisfaction. Whenever you try something new, there's always the chance that you're going to be embarrassing. But I was better than I thought I'd be. Not as good as I'd like to be, but I'm on my way. ⁓

Son

Long after I started this book, Son died. I'm not sure how to tell you about it, or if I should tell you, but I can't just ignore it. And what heading should it fall under? "My First (Real) Loss"? That doesn't sound quite right, because this was my only (real) loss. You think you've had many serious losses by the time you're my age, but then something happens that leaves you completely gutted. Only then do you understand what the word "loss" means.

It's like hearing the word "cancer." You hear people talk about it your whole life, but it's not until you sit across the desk from your doctor, while he looks you in your eyes and tells you that you have cancer, that you can truly understand this word!

As I try to write my feelings down about Son's death, it seems foolish to use my pen and paper. It feels like these words should be written in lightning or stone, some medium that reflects the magnitude of the event. I know this might sound corny or stupid, but when a tragedy hits you, the normal ways of communicating seem inadequate.

When you've known someone your entire life, you don't think of them being able to just leave you. Even if you're angry with one another, or you move to Africa, or they join some kind of religious cult, they're never just going to not be there.

That is how I felt about Son. In my life, at one time or another, he filled almost every role—father, brother, mentor, husband, partner, pain in the ass. In the beginning, he was my rock. He was the only one who truly understood about dreams—dreams to be someone different, someone better, respected, an artist! To not be satisfied to stay in your place, but to create a new place. These were the dreams that Son and I talked about endlessly. We planned, we pretended, we dreamt.

When we met, I was scared of everything, insecure, a child. He was tired of hitting his head against the showbiz wall, of being unhappily married, of being told that he had to grow up and give up dreaming. We were a match made in heaven—if not heaven, then in an old MGM musical. (One of the really good ones, overseen by Mr. Mayer himself.)

And now Son is dead.

I'd gotten into London late the night before. The phone woke me up around eight that Monday morning, or it could have been earlier—I don't think I ever knew what time it was after that.

The operator said, "We're sorry to disturb you, but your daughter's on the phone, and she says it's an emergency."

Then Chas got on the phone, and I said, "Da?" (That was her name in the family, from the time Elijah was little and we tried to get him to say "Chastity" by the syllables—*Chas-ti-ty*—and all he could say was, "Da-dee-da.")

Chas said, "Mom, Dad's dead."

I don't think the information really penetrated; I just got enough of it to make me go right into mother mode. I said, "Oh, sweetheart, I'm so sorry." I asked how it happened, and she said it was a skiing accident. And then I realized what we were actually talking about. And I stopped talking.

Chas said, "Mom, it'll be okay. Hang up the phone, Mom, I'm gonna have Georganne call you."

After a moment, I walked from my room to my assistant's room next door, and I stood there in the hallway knocking and crying. Jennifer opened the door, and held out the phone receiver to me. It was my sister, and I started to say, "Georganne"—and my legs went out from underneath me, and I was on my knees on the floor, sobbing hysterically.

I've had a couple of car accidents, and this felt the same way. At the start it's real quick, but then the center of it goes into slow motion.

You don't usually experience things happening fast and slow simultaneously, and its very difficult to keep your brain working for you.

I don't know how I did it, but I got ready and went to the airport. I cried myself to sleep on the airplane. I woke up and a Michael Douglas movie was playing. I watched it in some kind of daze. I remember thinking to myself, *This is good . . .*

But how could a movie be good now?

I started crying again, and then I fell back asleep, and that's what I kept doing for the rest of the flight.

I landed at LAX and went straight to Palm Springs. I was thinking, *It's good that I've pulled myself together, because this is going to be impossible for everybody, and I'm going to have to be the strong one.* I kept telling myself, over and over, *It's awful, it's a loss, but it's part of life, and we have to deal with it.* I'd done my homework, and I was on the other side of it. I'd be fine.

When I got to the house, I went into the kitchen and saw Christy, my stepdaughter. I thought she was going to cave in right away. But she didn't do what I thought she was going to do, and when we hugged, *I* started to cry.

I turned around toward the living room, and there were people I'd known my whole life. They came up and were hugging me, and that was a part of those next seven days—it was like a reunion, or a strange party. There was no pressure to sleep unless you felt like it, and if you got up and went to the kitchen, at any time of the day or night, someone was there. We'd make meat sauce for the pasta, and it felt so natural. And then we'd realize that the one thing missing was Son. He was the one who was supposed to be making the sauce.

At some point every day, it bit us in the ass, and we'd be sobbing. I'm not a person who cries around other people, but this was an exception. I knew everyone so well that I just didn't care.

On Wednesday morning, I got a visit from Denis Pregnolato, who was our friend and had worked with Son for years. There was lots of commotion going on in my room in the guest house. Elijah and Chas and her closest girlfriends were there, and a bunch of kids were running around—Mary's kids and their best friends, and Christy's son, Nico—and we were trying to explain to them why they couldn't play outside in the courtyard, because the paparazzi were hiding out and taking pictures through the bushes.

And Denis took me aside, and he said, "We all want you to do the eulogy."

I said, "Den, I'm not sure I can do it." What kept running through my head was, *I'm not sure I can do it good enough.*

Den said, "Everybody in the family wants you to do it."

I said I would do it, because I knew that Sonny would have dropped everything to do my eulogy if the tables had been turned.

My life was hell from that moment on. For the next forty-eight hours, I never had a moment's peace. I stayed in my room by myself almost all the time, writing and writing and writing, and throwing pages from a yellow legal pad every fucking place. I went through two pads before I had what I wanted, and then I went through another twenty-five pages, changing things around, or trying to think of something better.

I wanted to tell people about someone they didn't really know. I didn't want anyone to think that Son was stupid, because I know that had bothered him sometimes. When we were young, a lot of people looked at the way we dressed, and they blew us off as Neanderthals. I was definitely unpolished and pretty naïve, but Son was the person who made Sonny and Cher possible. When he played the fool on our TV show, it was just a part of our act. Son had created the act, and he was confident enough to let people laugh at him being silly or screwy.

He loved to make people laugh.

On Wednesday night, we had a private wake. I remembered what Son said to me the night before his grandmother's funeral—that it was better not to look at an open casket, and to keep the memories of the living person in your mind. I didn't want to look at Son. I was afraid. I didn't want to remember him any other way than the picture of him that I had in my mind.

Near the end of the wake, Chas said she wanted to go up to the casket. I asked her not to go, but she said, "Mom, I want to do this." So she did, but it was hard for her. She was up there alone, while everyone else was filing out, and finally I felt that I needed to go up and stand with her, no matter what. I remember approaching the casket with fear. How I didn't want to see Son inside that wooden box!

I looked down at his face, but I didn't see anything there. My mind's eye had an indelible picture of Son that will never change. It was so strong that nothing could destroy it, not even that casket.

Then I looked down at his hands. Sonny had the most beautiful, unbelievable hands. Now they were clasped on his chest, and seeing them made it all real for me.

As we got closer to Friday, I got more and more scared about the eulogy. I kept crying the whole time I was writing and re-writing it. I'm used to being in control of my exterior, keeping a deadpan expression. It's something that's stood me in good stead when I'm out in public. But now my facial muscles were working on their own, and I couldn't make them do what I wanted them to do.

Before Son and I went onstage, I used to say to him, "Son, what will happen if I get on and I need to get off—can I leave?" On that Friday morning, I kept asking my daughter: "What will happen, Chas—what's going to happen?" If I couldn't do what I was supposed to do, what would happen?

Chas started telling me that I would be all right. I was trying to listen to her, but I was so nervous, I just couldn't. I said, "Yeah, Chas, but *what will happen?* What will happen if I just get hysterical and I can't do it?"

She said, "Mom, you're a professional. When you get up there and start, you'll be fine. You'll do what you have to do."

But this wasn't an acceptance speech, or a lecture, or a movie, or a play. It didn't fit into any category. And I kept thinking, *What if I cannot speak?*

I kept studying what I'd written and making changes to the last minute. I changed every line—instead of "he used to talk," I'd think "he always talked" would sound better. Thank God the funeral was that morning, because I was driving myself insane.

I'd never written anything down for a speech before. I just got out there and said what came into my head. But this time I was worried that I'd wander all over the place, so I had to write it all down, word for word, so I could memorize it.

It had to be as perfect as I could make it.

But then I realized that I couldn't memorize the eulogy, after all. I just couldn't lock the words down in my mind.

It was time! We all walked into the church through a side door. I looked up and saw lots of lights in the back. I thought they'd let the press in for still pictures. I had no idea the funeral was going out live on CNN. When I found out about it later, I almost passed out.

I had to separate myself from my job that day. It was like I had to split myself down the middle. But then I took three steps toward the podium, and I got hysterical anyway. I thought, *This is not a good start— I've got to get ahold of myself.* I sucked up a deep breath, because I was so afraid that I wouldn't be able to say the words I needed to say.

Then I remembered hearing about an old Judy Garland trick. Whenever she was scared, she would lock her knees. So that morning I locked out my knees as I stood at the podium. I was shaking like a leaf.

I looked at my notes, which I'd written down really carefully. It hadn't occurred to me that I wouldn't be able to read them without my reading glasses. (The same kind that I'd always kidded Son about. I'd told Chas to tell her father, "Dad, Mom says you've got to change your glasses—you look like Mr. Magoo." But she wouldn't do it.)

But when I looked up to talk to the congregation, they all became a mishmash, so I kept taking the glasses off to see the people, and putting them back on to look at my notes.

The toughest part of the eulogy was the last part. Son had always reminded me of a section in *Reader's Digest* that I used to read when I was young: "The Most Unforgettable Character I Ever Met."

For me, that person was Salvatore Phillip Bono.

There was a point up on that podium when I didn't think I'd make it through to the end. And I thought to myself, *I don't care what you do, but you're going to get through this.* I bit the inside of my cheek so hard that I drew blood, but I got through the eulogy. It wasn't quite the job that I'd wanted to do, but I think people knew what I meant.

After Son and I split up, I would always say that leaving him was the toughest thing I would ever have to face. But that turned out to be not exactly true. The toughest thing was him leaving me.

That morning at the cemetery, just before Son was buried, I walked up to the coffin and placed my hand on it.

And I remember thinking, *This is not good-bye.*

PHOTO CREDITS